CHRISTIAN HEROES: THEN & NOW

CAMERON TOWNSEND

Good News
in Every Language

CHRISTIAN HEROES: THEN & NOW

CAMERON TOWNSEND

Good News in Every Language

JANET & GEOFF BENGE

YWAM
PUBLISHING

P.O. BOX 55787   SEATTLE, WA 98155

YWAM Publishing is the publishing ministry of Youth With A Mission. Youth With A Mission (YWAM) is an international missionary organization of Christians from many denominations dedicated to presenting Jesus Christ to this generation. To this end, YWAM has focused its efforts in three main areas: (1) training and equipping believers for their part in fulfilling the Great Commission (Matthew 28:19), (2) personal evangelism, and (3) mercy ministry (medical and relief work).

For a free catalog of books and materials, call (425) 771-1153 or (800) 922-2143. Visit us online at www.ywampublishing.com.

Cameron Townsend: Good News in Every Language
Copyright © 2000 by YWAM Publishing

Published by YWAM Publishing
a ministry of Youth With A Mission
P.O. Box 55787, Seattle, WA 98155

Sixth printing 2011

ISBN 13: 978-1-57658-164-3; ISBN 10: 1-57658-164-0

Printed in the United States of America

CHRISTIAN HEROES: THEN & NOW

Adoniram Judson
Amy Carmichael
Betty Greene
Brother Andrew
Cameron Townsend
Clarence Jones
Corrie ten Boom
Count Zinzendorf
C. S. Lewis
C. T. Studd
David Bussau
David Livingstone
D. L. Moody
Elisabeth Elliot
Eric Liddell
Florence Young
George Müller
Gladys Aylward
Hudson Taylor

Ida Scudder
Isobel Kuhn
Jacob DeShazer
Jim Elliot
John Wesley
John Williams
Jonathan Goforth
Lillian Trasher
Loren Cunningham
Lottie Moon
Mary Slessor
Nate Saint
Paul Brand
Rachel Saint
Rowland Bingham
Sundar Singh
Wilfred Grenfell
William Booth
William Carey

Unit study curriculum guides
are available for select biographies.

Available at your local Christian
bookstore or from YWAM Publishing
1-800-922-2143 / www.ywampublishing.com

Central America

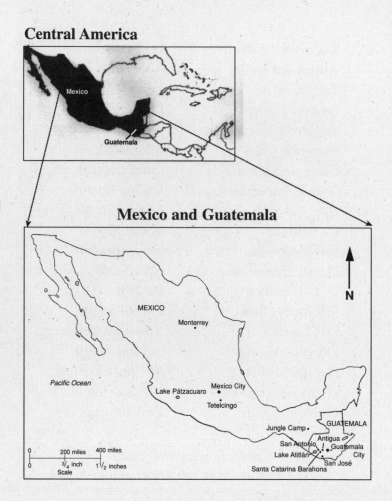

Mexico and Guatemala

MEXICO

Monterrey

Pacific Ocean

Lake Pátzacuaro

Mexico City

Tetelcingo

Jungle Camp

GUATEMALA

San Antonio

Antigua

Lake Atitlán

Guatemala City

Santa Catarina Barahona

San José

N

| 0 | 200 miles | 400 miles |
| 0 | 3/4 inch | 1 1/2 inches |

Scale

Contents

The Oval Office

Cameron Townsend sat on the couch and looked around. He found it hard to believe he was seated in the Oval Office of the White House. Across the room, behind a beautifully handcrafted desk sat President Richard Nixon, his craggy gaze fixed on Cameron.

It wasn't the first time Cameron Townsend had been in the presence of a president. On the contrary, he had met with numerous presidents and leaders around the world. A former president of Mexico had even become his close friend. But somehow, being in the presence of the president of the United States was different. Many Americans dreamed all their lives of meeting the president, and now Cameron Townsend sat less than ten feet from him.

After he had been introduced to President Nixon, Cameron explained that workers with Wycliffe Bible Translators, the organization he'd started, had just begun translating the Bible into its five hundredth language.

President Nixon looked very impressed. He leaned across his desk and looked Cameron in the eye. "What an achievement!" he exclaimed. "You are doing two wonderful things: giving people the Bible in their own language and teaching them to read it. What can I do to help you?"

Cameron took a deep breath. The president wanted to help him! It was more than he could have hoped for. He chose his words carefully. "Mr. President," he began, "we still have a lot of work to do. Even today there are over two thousand language groups that do not have an alphabet, much less a Bible translation. We need eighty-five hundred new recruits to get the job done. Would you be kind enough to write a letter that we can use to challenge young people all over this nation to volunteer their services?"

President Nixon's eyes lit up, and the corners of his mouth curled in a smile. "I would be honored to," he replied.

Cameron shook President Nixon's hand, and then their meeting was over. Cameron took one last look around at the plush surroundings of the Oval Office before being led from the room. After some of the places he had lived over the years, from a cornstalk hut to a tent, it was hard for him to imagine what it would be like to live in a mansion like the White House. Yet Cameron Townsend would not have traded one night living in a hut or a tent for a night in the White House. His living conditions may have been less than basic at times, but he had always been pursuing his lifelong dream. Besides, position, power, and prestige were not important to him. What was important was that people who had never had the chance to read the Bible in their own language got that opportunity. And that was the reason he had come to the White House to meet the president.

It was a snowy, blustery day outside when Cameron walked away from the White House. As he walked, he looked towards the Capitol and thought back to growing up in Southern California. His fellow students in high school had been convinced he would end up a senator within ten years. But what a different turn his life had taken. Yet as a missionary and a linguist, he had probably met more world leaders than he ever would have met as a senator. He wondered whether any of his boyhood friends back in Downey could have foreseen the twists and turns his life would take. Cameron Townsend certainly hadn't. Yet he wouldn't have changed the course of his life for anything.

Chapter 2

A Trip to Fresno

The crowing of a rooster woke fourteen-year-old Cameron Townsend early one morning in July 1910. As the early light of dawn filtered into the tiny room he shared with his brother Paul, Cam, as everyone called him, tried to remember why today was so special. Suddenly it came to him. Today he was going to Fresno with his mother and Paul. His four older sisters, Oney, Ethel, Lula, and Mary, wouldn't be going. They all had more important things to do than visit relatives in Fresno. They had jobs and boyfriends and other responsibilities they could not leave. And Cam's father, Will Townsend, would also be staying behind on the small farm the family rented. He had to tend to the tomato crop that would be ripe for picking in less than a month. After the harvest, he would make several trips into Los Angeles to sell his tomatoes at the farmers' market.

Until now, riding along on the wagon to Los Angeles with his father was the most exciting thing Cam could imagine. After all, Los Angeles was ten miles away. Today, though, things were going to change. He was about to ride a train two hundred twenty miles north to Fresno. Not only had he never ridden on a train before, but the farthest he'd been away from the farm was Long Beach, fourteen miles south of Downey. Each year the family went there on an outing to watch the ships pass by and wade in the cold water of the Pacific Ocean.

After rubbing the sleep from his eyes, Cam dropped his feet with a thud onto the polished wood floor. He was anxious to get his chores done and be on his way. He pulled back the threadbare floral curtain that separated the "bedroom" from the living room and scurried through the kitchen, where his father was sitting in the old rocking chair to the left of the stove, exactly the same place he sat every morning. His father was reading his Bible, just as he always did—three chapters on a weekday morning, five on Sunday. Cam waved to him as he grabbed a bucket and headed to the water pump for a morning wash. The wash taken care of, he quickly pulled on his coveralls and went to help his father milk the cows.

"Morning, boy," said Mr. Townsend in a very loud voice.

Cam turned his head so that his father could read his lips. "Good morning, Dad," he replied deliberately before squatting on a three-legged stool beside a cow. He rested his forehead against the animal's warm flank, reached for the udder, and began working his hands up and down. Cam aimed the flow of milk into a wooden pail. There was no talking with his father as he worked; there never was, since Will Townsend was stone-deaf. Cam's mother told Cam that it had happened gradually, the result of a construction accident back in Colorado soon after Cam's father had married Cam's mother. Cam's father could read lips and still liked to talk and sing, though he had no idea of how soft or loud his voice was.

Soon the pail was filled with creamy warm milk, and Cam and his father walked back to the tiny ramshackle farmhouse in which all eight members of the Townsend family lived. Mrs. Townsend had already made the oatmeal for breakfast, and Paul had set the table. Cam's older sisters emerged two at a time from their bedroom, and soon the whole family was seated around the table. Mr. Townsend gave thanks for the food, and they all began to eat.

After breakfast, Mary and Oney cleared away the dishes while Lula pulled the big leather Bible down from the shelf on the sideboard. Everyone sat silently as Mr. Townsend read a chapter from the Bible, and then they sang a hymn. It was "Amazing Grace," one of Mr. Townsend's favorites, which he sang with gusto. Cam and Paul looked at each other, barely able to keep themselves from laughing out loud at how off-key their father was singing. One look from their mother, though, was enough to snap them back into line. While she enjoyed a joke as much as anyone, the children were under strict orders never to laugh at their father. Everyone deserves his dignity and the chance to make the best of what he has, she would constantly tell them.

Finally Mr. Townsend offered up a prayer and finished the morning devotion with the same words as always: "May the knowledge of the Lord cover the earth as the waters cover the sea."

"Amen," chimed the entire family, and then the two boys were released from the table to pack the scuffed black duffel bag their mother had brought down from the attic for them.

Within an hour, Cam and Paul were seated in the back of the wagon. Once everyone was comfortable, Mr. Townsend cracked the reins, and the horse lunged forward, dragging the wagon behind. They bumped along towards the railway station to catch the eleven o'clock train north to Fresno.

Cam and Paul sat side by side, their noses pressed to the window, staring out as the train wound its way across the San Gabriel Mountains and on into the broad, fertile San Joaquin Valley.

"Twins?" asked the conductor as he came through the carriage collecting tickets.

"No," replied Mrs. Townsend. "Just two peas in a pod."

And so they were. While Cameron was two years older and a little taller than Paul, sitting down they looked almost identical. Paul's hair was a lighter shade of brown, and his eyes were brown, too, not blue like Cameron's. Apart from that, the two brothers looked pretty much alike with their side-parted hair, wide foreheads and slightly sticking out ears. But while they may have looked alike, they had very different interests. Cam liked to figure things out. He liked puzzles, mystery stories, riddles, and anything else that made him think hard. Paul, on the other hand, liked to do things with his hands. He was forever peering under the hood of the few automobiles that had started appearing around Downey, trying to understand how the pistons or carburetor worked.

The train rolled on through the lush countryside. Fields blooming with crops ready for harvest seemed to stretch on forever in every direction. Finally, at five o'clock in the afternoon, the train hissed to a stop at the station in Fresno. Mrs. Townsend let out a little gasp of happiness as she waved out the window. Cam leaned over to see what she was looking at and recognized his aunt and grandfather from the family photo that hung on the living room wall back at the farmhouse.

Soon everyone was standing on the station platform, where there was a lot of kissing and hugging. Cam was greatly relieved when it was time to climb into the wagon and head for his aunt and uncle's house. He liked his cousins instantly, and they all ran outside to explore the neighborhood while the adults sat drinking coffee and talking about how the prices for produce were better in 1910 than they had been the previous year and how wonderful it was that there was enough money left over for train tickets.

Fresno in July was much hotter than Downey, and Cam was glad his sister Ethel had made him a new swimsuit for his birthday on July 9, the week before the trip. The cousins wasted no time in showing Cam and Paul the local swimming hole, located in a nearby irrigation canal. Cam watched in admiration as his cousins leapt into the water, yelling and daring each other to go farther out. Finally they began calling for Cam to dive in. Cam swallowed hard, wondering how he was going to tell them he couldn't swim. After a few moments of indecision, he decided not to tell them at all. Instead, his heart beating wildly, he stepped back for a long run up to his dive. He had seen the others all dive, and it didn't look too difficult. He would just have to be careful not to go out over his head.

Cam dived off the edge of the canal, hitting the water at a steep angle. Water rushed up his nose and into his ears. He kicked his feet downwards, feeling for the bottom of the canal with his toes, but there was nothing. He needed air. Desperately he flailed around with his feet as he sank farther down. Finally his toes felt the silty bottom. With all his might he pushed off the bottom and shot upwards. As his head broke the surface of the canal, he had just enough time to take a half-choked breath and yell for help before he began to sink again. Down he went. Fear pulsed through him. He knew he was going to drown right there at age fourteen. Somehow he managed to take his mind off the fear and focus on his decision the year before to become a Christian. He was glad he had made the decision, though he hadn't planned on seeing heaven quite this soon.

Again his feet touched the bottom, and he was able to propel himself upward once more. He broke the surface and again yelled for help, though not so loudly this time. The water felt like it was surging into him through his nose and mouth, and he knew he didn't have the energy to fight to get to the surface again. His arms stopped flailing as he floated downwards. Everything was silent and still.

Suddenly Cam felt a strong hand grasp his hair and tug him towards the surface. He saw sunlight, and his mind told him it was okay to take a deep breath. Cam coughed and spluttered as he did so.

"He's here. I think he's okay," Cam heard his oldest cousin yell. Then Cam crawled up the bank and vomited.

For a long time, Cam lay in the sun at the edge of the canal. The thought of nearly drowning took a little adjusting to. Until now he'd never thought much about dying, but only moments ago it had been a real possibility. Cam decided not to go back in the water that day and instead walked back to his aunt's house. As he walked, thoughts about living and dying tumbled around in his head. The rest of the visit in Fresno passed uneventfully. Cam confessed to the others that he could not swim, and he never tried to go out over his head again.

The experience made Cam feel older and wiser. It also changed the way he thought about school. Until then he had coasted along, not really caring whether he got A's, B's, or even C's on his report card. However, when he went back to school that fall, Cameron Townsend had a goal. He was going to do his best and become a schoolteacher. He studied hard and came out at the top of his class.

Studying hard often wasn't enough in 1910. Many children had to drop out of school after eighth grade and get a job. It looked like Cam would be one of them. His parents did all they could to pay the family's bills, but they struggled desperately just to make ends meet. Finally Cam decided it was his duty to start earning a wage to help out the family. His sisters, though, would not hear of it. Lula, who was planning to marry that summer, insisted on putting the wedding off a year so that she could keep working as a secretary and give most of her income to her parents, freeing Cam to go on to ninth grade.

Lula's fiancé was not happy about the arrangement. He could not see any reason why a fourteen-year-old boy should still be attending school and why Cam's older sister felt obliged to pay for him to go. When he could not change Lula's mind about helping support her family, he broke off the engagement.

Before Cam started ninth grade, Lula was offered a better job in Santa Ana, and so over the summer, the whole family moved to a farm nearby. In Santa Ana Cam enrolled in ninth grade and continued to work very hard at his studies. He also began attending a local Methodist Sunday school. His teacher, Eugene Griset, wasted no time in visiting his newly arrived student. Then his visits became more frequent; he even began visiting when Cam was out.

Something was going on, which Cam soon figured out. Eugene might have said he was coming to visit Cam, but the person he really hoped to see was Lula! Soon Eugene and Lula began dating, and at the end of Cam's ninth year of school, the two were married. Once again the family moved, this time to Clearwater, where Cam enrolled at Compton High. Cam's father was in a slightly better financial position now, so Cam was able to attend Compton High from tenth through twelfth grade.

Even while attending school, Cam tried hard to make money whenever he could. He got a job hauling a group of other students who also lived in outlying areas to school in a wagon. He was responsible for driving the wagon in all weather, and he was paid seventy dollars a month from the school board for doing so. It sounded like an enormous amount of money until Cam discovered he had to feed and house the horses out of the money. He gave any money left over at the end of the month to his parents, who were grateful for his hard work.

Cam continued to excel at school. He played the lead in the school production, edited the 1914 yearbook, joined the debating team, and won a tennis championship. His whole family had sacrificed to get him this far, and Cam was determined to make the most of the opportunity. When the grades were added up at the end of his twelfth-grade year, Cam topped the class. However, he couldn't be the official valedictorian, since he had transferred into the school.

Nineteen fourteen was an uncertain year to graduate from high school. England and France had just declared war on Germany. Europe was in an uproar. Who knew what might lie ahead for the United States?

Cam also was uncertain about his future. He began having serious doubts about becoming a teacher, and by the time he had graduated, he had something else in mind.

Chapter 3

Discharged

Cam Townsend stood at the gate to Occidental College, a Presbyterian liberal arts school in Los Angeles. It was the fall of 1914, and he was about to begin college. Over the summer after graduating from high school, he had worked as a bellhop aboard the S.S. *President*, a steamship that plied the waters between San Diego and Vancouver, Canada. The job had been an eye-opening experience. The crew had come from many countries and backgrounds, and they laughed at and teased Cam because he was so naive. Cam, though, didn't mind. He was earning money, money that along with a partial scholarship from the Presbyterian Church would get him through college, as long as he was frugal.

The future laid out for Cam seemed as straight and well-defined as the neatly paved path that led to the main office of Occidental College. At the end of twelfth grade, Cam had made up his mind to be a Presbyterian pastor, and he hadn't had a single doubt since. Becoming a pastor would involve four years of study at Occidental College before going on to seminary for his final training.

As he swung the gate open and walked up the path, Cam recalled how pleased his family had been at the news. His sisters had all agreed to give a little extra money to support their parents so that Cam could be free to study without worrying about their welfare.

Everything went much as planned at Occidental College. During his first year, Cam took general courses and Spanish. He joined the debating team and made many friends, including Carroll Byram and Elbert Robinson. "Robby," as Elbert Robinson was called by everyone, was ten years older than Cam and was the head of the college's branch of the YMCA. He was also a very enthusiastic member of the Student Volunteer Movement (SVM), an organization that challenged the best and brightest students to go overseas, especially to China and India, as missionaries. In fact, the SVM had sent out over ten thousand missionaries, which represented nearly half of all Protestant missionaries in the world. Out of respect, Cam always listened politely when Robby talked about the Student Volunteer

Movement, but he wasn't particularly interested, since he knew his future lay in America.

During the summer following his freshman year, Cam took a job as a magazine salesman. He hated every minute of it. He wished he were back aboard the S.S. *President,* where he earned a steady paycheck. Somehow, though, he managed to save enough money to go back to college for another year.

Soon after Cam began his second year of study, John R. Mott, the leader of the Student Volunteer Movement, came to speak at Occidental College. Of course, Robby invited Cam to go along and hear him. Cam accepted the invitation, reasoning that since he was going to be a pastor it was his job to be informed about what was happening in the rest of the world. Instead of being a spectator, though, Cameron Townsend found himself drawn into the spirit of the gathering.

After the meeting, Cam signed up to become a member of the Student Volunteer Movement, not necessarily as a foreign missionary but as a person who was willing to consider it. To become part of the group, new members had to say why they wished to join. Cam, who normally had no difficulty putting his thoughts into words, was unable to come up with an intelligent answer. All he managed to write was, "I'm not sure why I wish to belong."

The following day, Robby gave Cam a copy of a book titled *Hudson Taylor in the Early Years: The Growth of a Work of God.* Cam read the book from cover to cover and decided that if he ever wanted to be a missionary, he would want to be like Hudson Taylor. Hudson Taylor had put aside his own culture to dress and live like the Chinese people he was trying to reach with the gospel.

When Cam told the family he was willing to consider being involved in foreign missions, they were not at all happy. Cam's mother's eyes filled with tears. "Aren't there enough challenges right here in America for you, son?" she asked.

Cam did not know how to answer her. Besides, the whole question of his future had become moot. It was 1916 and the United States was gearing up to enter the First World War. President Woodrow Wilson was trying his hardest to keep the United States from becoming involved in European affairs, but most people, including Cam, felt it was inevitable that the country would eventually be drawn into the war.

As the prospect of involvement in the war grew, Cam and his friend Carroll Byram decided the smartest thing to do was join the military before they were drafted. By doing so, they would have some choice as to who would train them and what they would do. Both men chose to join the National Guard. Carroll Byram was particularly interested in the engineering training the National Guard offered, and although Cam was not drawn to engineering, he thought the two of them should stick together.

While he waited to see what would happen with the war in Europe, Cam moved in with his parents at the small house and plot of land they had rented nearby. Money was tight during his third year at college, and living back at home with his parents was a way he could conserve the few dollars he had left. In his spare time, Cam helped his father plant and harvest barley as well as harvest the wild oats that grew on the vacant land next door.

Will and Molly Townsend had not yet adjusted to the idea that their oldest son might choose to become a missionary over being a pastor in the United States. As a result, Cam found himself writing many notes to his father trying to explain the vague feeling he had that he should be prepared to go as a missionary if need be. Because of his father's deafness, notes were the best way for Cam to explain his feelings. However, after each note, his father kept pushing for details. Because Cam had no specific details, just a vague feeling, in the end he wrote his father a note saying, "The greater need is where the greatest darkness is." His father nodded in understanding. He had ended every prayer Cam could remember with the same words: "May the knowledge of the Lord cover the earth as the waters cover the sea." He now knew that his son wanted a tiny part in making that prayer become a reality. Cam was relieved that at last his father understood his interest in becoming a missionary.

Not long afterwards, in January 1917, Cam heard of an interesting opportunity that would test his commitment to missions. The Bible House of Los Angeles was advertising for people who would sell

Bibles in remote tribal areas in Central and South America. Since Cam thought he might like to do that the following summer, he replied to the advertisement. Within a week he received a letter telling him he had been accepted as a Bible salesman in Guatemala. Cam had no idea where Guatemala was, so he pored over an old map until he found it. Guatemala turned out to be a small country located right next to Mexico at the top of Central America. Cam stared at the map for a long time, trying to imagine what it would be like in Guatemala.

Three months later, in April 1917, his plan to go to Guatemala didn't seem to matter. The United States had finally entered the war in Europe, and it would be only a matter of time before Cam and Carroll Byram were called up and sent off to fight. Given this, it was quite unexpected when Mr. Smith, director of the Bible House of Los Angeles, contacted Cam to tell him a Miss Stella Zimmerman wanted to meet him. Stella was a missionary from Guatemala who was visiting the Los Angeles area.

"There's no point," Cam told Mr. Smith politely. "I just heard from my commander, and we are all going to be shipped off to France soon."

Mr. Smith didn't miss a beat. "Why don't you meet her anyway? It can't do any harm, since she's in the area. The war won't last forever. It's an opportunity you shouldn't miss."

When Mr. Smith put it that way, Cam didn't have the heart to refuse, and so a meeting was arranged for the following evening.

As the following day passed, Cam began to regret agreeing to the meeting. He convinced Robby Robinson to go to the meeting with him in case he ran out of things to say to some old spinster missionary. When he finally arrived at the meeting, Cam was surprised to discover that Stella Zimmerman was only about thirty years old. She was tall and willowy and had striking blonde hair. After greeting Cam and Robby, she launched right into a conversation about Guatemala. She painted such vivid word pictures of the place that Cam found himself wishing he were going there instead of France.

When Stella had finished telling them all about the tribes in Guatemala who had never had the gospel presented to them in their own language, she looked straight into Cam's eyes. "When will you be arriving?" she asked.

Cam had been dreading telling her he wouldn't be going at all. He wished he had told her straight out when he'd introduced himself. Now he felt very uncomfortable as he searched for the right words. Before he managed to get anything out, Robby came to his rescue. "Cam was interested in going, but he's a corporal in the National Guard, and his unit has been called up." When Stella looked at Robby with a look that asked, What about you?, he quickly added, "I'm thinking of applying for officer training school myself. We both want to do our part for the war effort."

Stella looked indignant. "What cowards!" she exclaimed. "You would go off to war where there are already millions of men fighting and leave women to carry on the Lord's work! God needs you in Central America!"

Both men sat in uncomfortable silence. What could they say? It was true, there were now thousands of men being shipped off every day to Europe to fight. Yet Cam knew there was nothing he personally could do about it. It would have been different if he had met Stella before he'd signed up for the National Guard, but now it was too late.

Finally, Robby turned to Cam." How about it, partner? What do you say we go to Central America?"

Cam stared back at his friend wondering if he was crazy. There was no way he could go anywhere. "I'm due to leave any day now, and I've never heard of an able-bodied person being discharged," he finally spluttered.

Robby put his hand on Cam's arm. "Let's pray that you do!" he said, his eyes shining brightly.

Cam didn't know what to say. In the end he said weakly, "Well, if that's what God wants, I'm willing."

Robby and Stella grinned at each other as if they had planned it all along. Cam, though, just thought they were both carried away with enthusiasm. There was no way he could get out of going to France to fight.

Having said he was willing to go to Guatemala if discharged from the National Guard, Cam felt obliged to ask for a discharge, even though he knew it would be turned down. His history professor helped him write a letter to the captain of the local National Guard unit.

Cam was certain the captain would roll his eyes and say he'd seen it all now. But the captain did not. He read the letter through once, and then a second time. He stood thinking for a minute and then turned to Cam. "Go," he said. "You'll do a lot more good selling Bibles in Central America than you will shooting Germans in France!"

Cam stared blankly at the captain, trying to take in his words. "Go?" he finally stammered incredulously. "A discharge, sir? You mean you'll sign my discharge?"

The captain laughed out loud. "That's what I said, isn't it?"

Cam nodded in delight. He could hardly wait to tell Robby. They were going to Guatemala after all!

Chapter 4

Mr. Jesus

The whistle of the S.S. *Peru* pierced the early morning air as Cam and Robby stood on deck watching the docks of San Francisco glide by. It was September 15, 1917, and they were finally on their way to Guatemala. Cam thought back over the previous months. It hadn't been easy to get this far, but once he received his discharge papers, nothing could stop him. Though the Bible House of Los Angeles would pay them each thirty dollars a month once they reached Guatemala, Cam and Robby had needed to raise one hundred fifty dollars each for their fares. To raise the money, they had spent the summer on a ranch pitching hay and planting corn. It was backbreaking work, but they broke the monotony of it by quizzing each other on

Spanish vocabulary. As they worked they waited to see whether Robby would be drafted into the army to fight in Europe. Since he hadn't been called up so far, he and Cam were both free to leave the country.

Cam and Robby had traveled north to San Francisco to catch the ship. Since the war effort had put a strain on shipping, the few ships that still traveled between the West Coast of the United States and Central and South America mostly left from San Francisco. When they arrived there, Cam and Robby discovered that the only passenger ship headed south anytime soon had only first-class cabins available. The two men had planned on staying in a cheap tourist-class cabin deep in the bowels of the ship and did not have the extra money to cover a first-class fare. Undeterred, they set about earning the extra money they needed. They stayed in a cheap boarding house near the docks and took jobs loading crates onto ships for the Wells Fargo Company. They were paid fifteen dollars a week, and they saved every penny of it they could. To save money, they ate poached eggs for breakfast, lunch, and dinner. By the time they were done, Cam never wanted to see another poached egg in his life. Still, they had managed to save the extra money they needed for their fares. It had been hard work, but it paled in significance when compared to the adventure that lay ahead of them.

As the steam-driven propeller churned the waters of San Francisco Bay and gently pushed the S.S. *Peru* along, twenty-one-year-old Cameron

Townsend turned and grinned at his friend. Robby was leaning against the rail, his foot resting on the small trunk he had brought aboard. Neither of them had been below deck yet to check out the first-class cabin they had worked so hard to pay for. They were too excited to go below and stow their belongings. Neither of them wanted to miss a thing.

Cam looked back towards the docks where the day's activities were beginning. Wagons filled with barrels and crates were being unloaded, and an army unit was assembling near a tin shed at the far end of one pier. Each soldier had a duffel bag slung over his shoulder. Cam supposed they were probably about to be shipped out to join the fighting in France, which was where all the action in the war seemed to be taking place. Cam thought about his friend Carroll Byram, who had been shipped off to France a month before. Carroll would probably be fighting there by now along with the other men in the National Guard unit Cam had trained with.

As a seagull swooped low overhead, Cam could hardly believe he was back at sea. Ever since his stint as a bellhop aboard the S.S. *President* three summers before, he had longed to be on the ocean again.

At dinner that night the captain told them it would take about twenty days to reach their destination. They would sail down the Baja California peninsula and then head southeast past the remainder of the western coast of Mexico and then on to

San José, Guatemala. Eighteen days later, and two days ahead of schedule, the S.S. *Peru* dropped anchor off the coast of San José.

"Hop in. You first, Cam," said the captain, eyeing Cam's scrawny 130-pound body and pointing to the large metal basket the ship's crane had lowered to the deck.

Cam did as instructed, and then Robby followed him into the basket.

The captain handed them their luggage. "Put this at your feet and sit on it. Got to keep the center of gravity low or you'll tumble out," he instructed.

Cam nervously peered through the slats in the side of the basket as he and Robby were jerked into the air by the crane and swung out over the handrailing. The basket was lowered, and soon Cam felt the bottom of it bump onto the deck of a lighter boat. Quickly the two men climbed out.

"Buenos días, señors," said one of the deckhands on the lighter boat as he reached into the basket and pulled out their bags.

"Good day to you, too," replied Cam in Spanish, realizing as he did so that the trip in the basket had transported him from an English-speaking world into a Spanish-speaking one.

The lighter boat rose and fell in the swell as it chugged its way into the harbor at San José. Once Cam and Robby were ashore, a crew member escorted them to the customs and immigration office, where their passports were inspected. The officer on duty hardly noticed their luggage.

"I guess we don't look the smuggling type," said Cam with a grin as the two men walked out of the office.

"I guess not," agreed Robby. Then looking at the size of his bag he added, "Couldn't fit much in there if we tried anyway."

"So far so good. We need to find a bank and exchange some money to buy tickets to Guatemala City," said Cam, looking around for a building with the word *Banco* on it.

Cam and Robby found a bank soon enough and then headed for the train station. Both men were grateful for the Spanish they had learned, but Cam was a little dismayed at how fast the locals spoke. "Repeat please" and "Slow down" became two of his most-used phrases.

From the giggles Cam got when he introduced himself to the woman sitting near him on the train, he suspected there was something wrong with his name. He pulled out his Spanish dictionary to find out what it was. No wonder the woman had laughed. "Cameron" sounded just like the Spanish word for shrimp! Right then and there Cam decided to do something about it. He was skinny enough as it was without introducing himself to everyone as Mr. Shrimp. Instead, he decided to use his first name in Spanish-speaking countries. He would be don Guillermo (Guillermo being Spanish for William, his first name).

Later that night, as the train pulled into the station at Guatemala City, a wave of relief swept over

Cam as he spotted Stella Zimmerman. Stella's tall, blonde figure was easy to see above the sea of dark heads. Stella greeted Cam and Robby and introduced them to a pastor who had accompanied her to the station. She told them they would be staying in an attic apartment belonging to Central American Mission.

It was eleven o'clock before a horse-drawn carriage dropped the two men off at the apartment. Edward Bishop, the director of Central American Mission (CAM) in Guatemala, was waiting downstairs to meet them. The Bible House of Los Angeles had asked him to keep an eye on the two raw recruits. After introducing themselves, Cam and Robby headed upstairs to their tiny apartment. Cam dropped his bag and flopped onto the bed, exhausted from all the traveling, while Robby unpacked all his shaving gear for the next morning. As Cam lay in bed, he could hear conversation wafting up from downstairs. He could make out Edward Bishop talking to another man about the work Robby and Cam would be doing. At one point, the other man laughed. "I think Robinson will do fine. He's the big fellow, right?" he said.

"Yes," agreed Edward Bishop.

The other man continued. "That skinny Townsend kid, though, won't last two months!"

Cam rolled over, trying not to hear anything else the men were saying. It had cost him a lot of money to get this far, and he was determined to last longer in Guatemala than two months.

The following morning, Cam and Robby met
with Edward Bishop, who explained that he already
had their first month planned out. They would
spend the first two weeks getting used to their new
surroundings: the food, the language, the customs.
They would then all head over the mountains to the
old capital of Antigua to attend a Bible conference.
This would give Cam and Robby an opportunity to
meet some local Christians. When the conference
was finished, they would collect a supply of
Spanish Bibles and head into the mountain regions.

It all sounded fine to Cam and Robby, who
enjoyed their time wandering around the streets of
Guatemala City, sampling the local food, and trying
out their limited Spanish.

The trip to Antigua two weeks later was not so
enjoyable. Before riding on ahead on horseback,
Edward Bishop had arranged for Cam and Robby
to be transported on a mule cart. As the cart
climbed up the western side of the mountain range,
rain began to pour down. The four mules pulling
the cart slowed to a crawl. The driver whipped
them mercilessly and yelled curses at the top of his
lungs. But no matter what he tried, he could not get
the mules to move any faster on the treacherous
trail. Indeed, the trail was so slippery that on some
corners, the wheels of the cart slid sideways, sending clods of mud shooting up over the passengers.
Once they finally reached the top of the mountain
range, the mules lunged down the other side,
careening around sharp turns. As Cam looked over

the edge of the steep cliffs that dropped away at the side of the trail, all he could do was to pray they would make it to Antigua alive.

They did, and Edward Bishop was waiting to show them to their room. It was a simple affair with just two army cots and a basin for washing. It suited Cam and Robby just fine. They knew their next stop in the mountains would be much more primitive.

The Bible conference proved to be an eye-opening experience. Cam had been told a little of the religious history of Guatemala. He knew the Spanish had invaded the country in 1523 and declared Roman Catholicism to be the only religion. Most of the country's two million Indians continued to practice their old Mayan religions along with the religion of their Spanish masters. Then in 1871, a revolution occurred that eventually brought to power General Justo Rufino Barrios. General Barrios was a reformer who opened the way for Protestant churches to come to Guatemala. He told people they were free to worship wherever they wanted, and the first public, non-Catholic schools were set up. The general went so far as to travel to New York City to ask the Presbyterian Church to send missionaries to his country. The church responded to the request and later joined forces with Central American Mission. All of this had happened over forty years before, but many government officials and citizens of Guatemala were still fiercely Roman Catholic and resented any Protestant group working in the country.

At the conference, Cam and Robby got to hear the testimonies of Guatemalan Protestant Christians. Cam could hardly believe what he heard. It was like reading from the book of Acts. One shoemaker told the group how he had been thrown into jail sixty-three times for drunkenness before being converted. Since then he had not been drunk again, but he had been thrown in jail three more times—those times for preaching the gospel. As others recounted stories of being beaten or stoned, Cam began to wonder what he had signed up for.

Finally, the last day of the conference arrived. At the meeting that morning, Edward Bishop spoke about the need for Christians to share their faith with others, even strangers. He urged all who were present to find someone to talk to about their faith that day. Cam gulped. He had been a Christian since he was twelve years old, and most of his friends were Christians. This was not because he had played any part in converting them, but because they had also been raised in Christian homes and had followed their parents' examples.

As he sat on a folding canvas chair in the meeting, Cam realized for the first time that he had never actually talked about his faith with a non-Christian. Here was Edward Bishop challenging him to share his faith in Spanish, and he had never even tried to do it in English! Worse still, he was a missionary! He wondered how he could have overlooked such an important point. Convinced he should remedy the situation right away, Cam slipped out when the meeting concluded for lunch. Somehow he had to find the right person to share his faith with.

It was not an easy task for Cam. His hands were sweaty, his heart beat wildly, and he had no idea how to start. He walked up to an old woman carrying a bag of sweet potatoes. A young boy accompanied her, and Cam decided he was going to talk to them about his faith. However, when he opened his mouth to speak, only little squeaking noises came out. Cam fled the scene, grateful in his embarrassment that he would never have to see the old woman or young boy again.

Finally, he calmed down enough to try again. This time he spotted a young man leaning against a storefront. Gingerly, Cam approached him. This time he knew what he was going to say; he'd been rehearsing it for a block. He would say, *¿Conoce usted al Señor Jesús?* which meant, "Do you know the Lord Jesus?" Relief flooded through Cam when he finally got the words out.

The young man frowned, obviously confused. Finally he responded. "I'm sorry, I don't know the man," he replied in Spanish as he shrugged his shoulders. He then added sympathetically, "I'm a stranger in town, too."

Cam felt himself turning red. He should have thought! Jesus was a common man's name in Spanish, and the young man had assumed Cam was looking for someone named Mr. Jesus somewhere in the city. Not knowing enough Spanish to untangle the confusion, Cam mumbled, "Thank you anyway," as he turned and fled once again.

Too embarrassed to return to the conference, Cam rushed to his room. He shut the door firmly behind him and sank to his knees beside his cot. "Lord, I'm a failure," he cried, wondering how he had managed to come so far without thinking about what being a missionary would entail. He wondered how he could face anyone again after the fool he'd just made of himself.

The next morning Cam was still disturbed about the events of the day before. He was glad when Edward Bishop called him and Robby into his office to give them their assignments. Cam was eager to get out of the city and into the countryside. Robby would be going north from Antigua to sell Bibles, while Cam would be going five miles southwest to sell Bibles around the towns of San Antonia Aguas Calientes and Santa Catarina Barahona. A tribe of Indians called the Cakchiquel lived in the area. Few if any Christians were among them, and many had never seen or heard of the Bible.

Not too many preparations had to be made before the two men parted. Tecpan, where Robby was headed, was about thirty miles to the north. Robby and Cam pooled their money to buy Robby a horse, which cost twenty-five dollars. One thing was for sure, Cam joked. Even though the horse was bony, it would provide a much less hair-raising journey for Robby than having to ride again on a mule cart.

The two friends parted on October 23, 1917. They agreed to meet each other in a month in nearby Santiago. Then they would travel together back to Guatemala City for Thanksgiving and to attend another of Edward Bishop's Bible conferences. Cam watched until Robby and his horse had disappeared from sight.

A local pastor, Isidro Alarcón, had offered to guide Cam across the coffee plantations to Santa Catarina Barahona. After Robby had departed, Cam hoisted the backpack filled with Spanish Bibles onto his back and carried his suitcase in his right hand. Isidro Alarcón, who was also carrying a supply of Bibles, led the way through the winding cobblestone streets of Antigua and out into the Guatemalan countryside. As Cam fell into step behind him, he wondered what he and Robby would be talking about in a month's time. After his failed attempts at sharing his faith the day before, he wasn't so sure he had much to say to the Cakchiquel Indians.

Chapter 5

On the Trail

When the trail widened, Isidro Alarcón and Cam walked side by side. Cam spoke first. "Are there any Christians among the Cakchiquel Indians?" he asked.

"Yes, and it's quite a story, don Guillermo," Isidro Alarcón replied, his eyes shining. "About eight months ago, a Cakchiquel man named Silverio Lopez was working in Guatemala City. Unlike most of the Cakchiquel, he could read and write a little Spanish, and so he bought a Bible in the city with which he hoped to improve his reading. Alas, he became discouraged and soon gave up trying to read the Bible. About then his wife sent a message saying their son had died and their daughter was very ill. Silverio Lopez quit his job and set out for home right away. In fact, he walked along this very trail."

Cam nodded. On the trail they had passed a number of Indian men dressed in their tunic shirts tied with a sash and worn over white pants that stopped just below their knees. Cam could easily imagine one of them being Silverio Lopez hurrying home to see whether his daughter was alive or dead.

The pastor continued. "Fortunately, his daughter was still alive when he got home, and so he went straight to the village witch doctor to find out what he should do to stop the evil spirits of his dead ancestors from killing her, too. The witch doctor told Silverio to buy candles and burn them in front of a specific image at the Catholic church. Silverio hurried to obey, convinced it would save his daughter.

"Despite his best efforts, his daughter got no better and hung between life and death. But then Silverio Lopez had another problem: debt. The witch doctor charged a lot of money for his advice, and the candles were not cheap either. Silverio also had to pay for his son's funeral. With no job and more candles to buy, he did not know what to do."

Cam fell back behind Pastor Alarcón as a mule train headed in the opposite direction passed them on the trail. Each mule had two enormous burlap pannier bags draped across it with two more sacks heaped on its back.

"Coffee beans," informed Isidro Alarcón, noticing Cam's inquisitive look.

When the mule train had passed, Cam prodded the pastor to continue with the story. "What happened next?" he asked.

"One day on his way back from the market, Silverio Lopez found a torn piece of paper. It had writing on it, so he picked it up and read the words. It was a quote from the Bible. It read, 'My house should be called a house of prayer, but you have made it a den of thieves.'

"Silverio thought about the words all the way home. He got out his Spanish Bible and looked the particular verse up. He then began reading the Bible again. It was difficult for him, but this time he persevered. By the next morning, he had decided what he would do. He stopped consulting the witch doctor, walked to Antigua to buy proper medicine for his daughter, and then came to find me."

"Why you?" asked Cam, mopping his brow with his handkerchief.

"Someone had told him I could teach him the Bible, so he showed up on my doorstep wanting to know how he could believe in the God of the Bible. I told him, and he decided to become a Christian right there in my living room. He went back to his Cakchiquel people and began reading the Bible aloud to them. That was six months ago," Isidro Alarcón chuckled. "Now there are forty new converts in the village!"

"What an amazing story!" exclaimed Cam, thinking again of his own failed efforts at sharing his faith.

By now they had reached the top of a hill. Spread below them was a beautiful sight—a wide, shallow valley rimmed with three volcanoes: Agua, Acatenango, and Fuego. A shining blue lake and two villages were located in the valley.

"That is Santa Catarina Barahona," said Pastor Alarcón, pointing toward the village on the right, "and the village on the left is San Antonia Aguas Calientes."

Cam stood for several minutes taking in the view. He wished his parents were there to see it, as it would be impossible to adequately describe the vista in a letter.

It was a quick descent to the valley floor, and an hour later Cam found himself being greeted by a short, barefoot Indian man. "My name is Francisco Díaz. Welcome in the Lord's name," he said in halting Spanish. "We have made you a bed in the chapel, but now I think you would be hungry."

Cam grinned. "Indeed I am," he replied.

"I will leave you now," said Pastor Alarcón. "I will visit with Silverio Lopez and then be on my way home."

When the pastor left, Francisco Díaz showed Cam to the chapel. It was a simple building. The walls were made from cornstalks lashed together in rows, and the roof was made of thatched straw. The floor was hardened dirt over which a woven mat had been laid. A row of rough-hewn pews filled the left side of the building. At the far end was a table covered with a cloth. Cam guessed it served as the pulpit.

Soon Francisco Díaz was busy making tortillas and heating chili soup over a smoky fire in the corner. As Cam watched, he became aware that other people were peering at him through the gaps in the cornstalk walls. Slowly he turned to them and smiled. "Please come in," he said.

Gradually the semidark building filled with Cakchiquel Indians. There were mothers with babies, toothless old men, and young boys and girls. The men sat on the pews while the women and children took their places sitting cross-legged on the floor.

A few minutes later, Silverio Lopez himself entered the chapel. He greeted Cam warmly and then lit a lamp. Seeing all the people who had come to welcome Cam, he decided it was a good time to hold a church service. He led the people in two hymns, sung in Spanish, and then invited Cam to the makeshift pulpit to preach. All this was unexpected to Cam, but he stood and told the group why he had come and quoted several verses from the Bible.

It was late before the last local Christians left the chapel and Cam was finally alone. He lay down on the mat-covered dirt floor and pulled a thin blanket over himself. The floor was hard, but Cam was tired, and within minutes he had fallen into a deep sleep.

The scratching of chickens around his feet awoke him with a start the following morning, and for a moment he had to think hard about where he was. Just then, Francisco Díaz popped his head in the door. "Good morning, don Guillermo. Are you ready for coffee?"

Cam sat up and rubbed his eyes. "Yes, thank you," he replied. "I'll be right out."

As the two men sat with their backs against the cornstalk side of the chapel sipping steaming hot coffee, Cam went over his plan for the day. He would start visiting each house in San Antonia Aguas Calientes, or San Antonio, as the locals shortened it to, offering the people in the houses Bible tracts and the opportunity to buy a Spanish Bible. However, Francisco Díaz forgot to tell Cam it was customary to stand at the gate and yell before entering a person's yard. After a mangy dog bit him on the leg, Cam quickly learned that custom.

A few people Cam visited bought Bibles from him, but most people were peasants who could not read or write in Spanish, and Cam had no Cakchiquel Bible to give them, since it was not a written language. This discouraged Cam, who wondered how anyone expected him to sell Bibles in Spanish to people who could not read or write the language. For three days he kept at it without making much headway. During the third day he stopped by a beer garden, an open area where men sat drinking alcohol. He asked whether anyone would like to buy a Bible or take a gospel tract. Some of the men just turned away, and a few jeered, but one man caught Cam's eye. The man walked over to Cam. "Would you like a tract?" Cam asked.

The man shook his head. "No sir," he replied, his voice slurred with alcohol. "I would take one, but what's the point? I can't read it."

Once again Cam wondered how to get the gospel message across when no one could read a Bible. He left the beer garden and walked on down the street towards another house. Ten minutes later he heard someone running behind him. He turned to see that it was the man who had refused the tract.

"Wait," yelled the man, waving his arms. "Please sir," he panted as he came closer. "I remember I have a friend who can read. Sell me one of your Bibles."

"Certainly," replied Cam, trying to conceal his excitement. "And why don't you come to the chapel on Sunday morning? I'll be speaking and will look out for you. What's your name?"

"Tiburcio," replied the man, who was now standing close enough for Cam to smell the liquor on his breath.

"Okay, Tiburcio," he said, handing over a Bible. "I'll see you on Sunday."

Sure enough, on Sunday morning when Cam surveyed the crowd of Cakchiquel Indians who had gathered in the chapel, there was Tiburcio sitting near the back of the room. He looked a little uncomfortable, but at least he had showed up. Cam was delighted.

The service lasted for over an hour, and as he preached, Cam watched the door to make sure Tiburcio did not slip out. When the sermon was over, he asked whether anyone in the room would like to become a Christian. Tiburcio leapt to his feet and hurried to the front. "Yes, I do," he said in a loud, clear voice.

As they prayed together, tears welled up in Cam's eyes, blurring his vision. In front of him stood a brand-new Christian, and he had played a part in the man's conversion. Maybe he wasn't a failure at sharing his faith after all.

Cam stayed in the valley for two weeks before heading west into the mountains. By then he had become good friends with Francisco Díaz and invited him to go along as guide. Francisco was eager to accompany Cam, but his coffee and corn were ready to harvest, and so several other Cakchiquel Christians filled in as guides for Cam.

It was an interesting two weeks in the mountains, and like the incident with the dog bite, Cam learned many lessons in his travels, most of them the hard way.

On November 1, All Saints' Day, Cam and his guide Lucas arrived in a village where people were milling around in the church cemetery. "Let's go over there," said Cam, fascinated by the sight and thinking of all the tracts he could hand out. As he came closer, he was astonished by what he saw. Plates of food, packets of cigars, and bottles of alcohol had been placed on top of the graves. "What is all that for?" he asked Lucas.

"It is for the spirits of the dead people," replied his guide matter-of-factly. "Today is the day the people believe their relatives come back from the dead. If the spirit of the dead person does not find gifts on his grave, he will put an evil curse on the family."

Cam sighed deeply. Guatemala was so steeped in superstition. He longed for people to read the Bible for themselves so they could discover the truth and free themselves from such burdensome practices.

In the mountain town of Chimaltenango, Cam and Lucas ran into real trouble. A band of local men surrounded them yelling, "Evangelistas!" and "Leave, you cursed Protestants!" The men carried sticks and grew angrier by the minute. Cam was praying hard under his breath when a contingent of soldiers arrived and broke up the mob. The soldiers escorted Cam and Lucas to the town hall, where the two men found temporary shelter.

Once the town hall doors were locked safely shut behind them, Cam wondered what he should do next. A group of very hostile people was outside, and only a few local officials were inside with him. With a flash of insight Cam knew exactly what he should do. "I would like to talk to the mayor," he said in his best Spanish.

Five minutes later, Cam and Lucas were sitting in the mayor's office. Cam noticed that the mayor looked nervous, but instead of complaining to him about the rough treatment he had received in his town, Cam began to tell him about the Bibles he wanted to sell there and the ways in which that could help the people of the town.

The mayor was impressed—and relieved. He arranged an official welcome for the two men. After the welcome, the mob that had been out to get the missionaries quickly evaporated, and many people took gospel tracts or bought Bibles.

As Cameron Townsend left Chimaltenango, he thought about his experience there and he made himself a promise: He would always try to gain the cooperation of the local authorities *before* going into a town, not after he'd already made enemies. Cam felt sure this was a key to working among the Cakchiquel Indians. What he did not know was that it would be a key that would open other doors and more opportunities than he could ever have dreamed possible.

Chapter 6

A Sudden Burst of Clarity

As planned, Cam met Robby in Santiago, and the two of them traveled back to Guatemala City for Thanksgiving. Cam was excited to hear all about Robby's experiences during the previous month. It was good to be talking to someone in English again. However, their time together was tinged with sadness. Waiting at Central American Mission headquarters was a letter to Cam from his mother. He eagerly opened it, only to find it contained the sad news that his close friend Carroll Byram had been killed on a battlefield in France. It seemed unbelievable to Cam that someone as lively and full of promise as Carroll could be dead, but the ongoing war was claiming the lives of a large number of young American men. Cam was sobered by how close he had come to being one of them.

Three days after arriving in Guatemala City, it was time for Cam and Robby to return to their work. This time they agreed to meet for Christmas. Cam was looking forward to the next month. Now that his coffee and corn were harvested, Francisco Díaz had agreed to accompany Cam as his guide.

When Cam arrived in Escuintla, a small town south of Guatemala City, Francisco Díaz was waiting for him as arranged. That night Francisco caught Cam up on all the news from the village. He told Cam how the men from the beer garden had poured liquor all over Tiburcio after he told them he had become a Christian. Tiburcio had also been slashed with a machete for proclaiming his faith in and around the village, but it had not stopped him from doing so. And since he was no longer spending his money on alcohol, Tiburcio had been able to pay back some of his debts. He also was working much harder now, and his boss had promoted him to foreman.

Cam was delighted with the news. That night he wrote in his journal, "It showed me that God could use even a poor instrument like myself when willing to be led...."

The following morning Cam and Francisco headed southwest towards the border of El Salvador. They stopped at over thirty villages as they went and talked to countless people. At least, Francisco Díaz did. Few of the Cakchiquel Indians in the area spoke Spanish, making it difficult for

Cam to have a conversation with any of them. The people also had no use for the Spanish Bibles Cam had with him. Indeed, one Indian man became indignant when Cam offered him a tract in Spanish. "Do you have one in Cakchiquel?" he asked.

"There are none. I'm sorry," replied Cam.

"Well," retorted the man, "if your God is so great, why can't he speak my language?"

Cam had no answer for him. He admired the Christians in the area learning Spanish just so they could read the Bible, but there were only a few of them. It was a difficult task learning to speak and read in another language, especially when there were no schools or teachers to help.

Cam ended up selling most of his Bibles to *Ladinos*. Ladino was the name for the Guatemalan people who were part Indian and part Spanish. Ladinos held the power in the country. They were well educated and owned huge *finca* (ranches) in the country. They were also the main businesspeople of the country. Generally, Ladinos looked down on Indian people. They saw the Indians as backward and unable to learn. But as Cam observed Francisco Díaz, he became convinced that the Cakchiquel Indians were as smart as anyone else. What they lacked were opportunities and a written language.

Throughout the month as Cam and Francisco trekked through the lush coffee plantations of southern Guatemala, the words of the indignant Indian man haunted Cam. Why didn't God speak Cakchiquel?

By December 23, 1917, Francisco Díaz had returned home for Christmas, and Cam had made his way back to Guatemala City to meet up with Robby. Cam and Robby had been invited to spend Christmas at the home of a Presbyterian missionary. It had been less than three months since they had arrived in Guatemala, but it felt like they had been in the country a lifetime, and they had much to talk about. They spent several hours sharing their observations of the main problems affecting the lives of the people they had visited. They decided that perhaps the biggest problem facing the Indians was the *mozo* system.

The mozo system was a complicated situation in which an Indian man would get into a position where he needed to borrow money. More often than not, the money was needed to buy liquor. The only people with money to lend were the owners of large finca, and most often they also owned the local liquor stores. Once an Indian owed money to a finca owner, a vicious cycle was set in motion. The Indian man went to work on the finca to earn money to pay back his debt. Sadly, he was away from his family and had to put in long hours of backbreaking labor. To take his mind off his situation, the man would begin to drink more. Of course, he then had to borrow more money to pay for the alcohol until he eventually owed so much to the finca owner that he was virtually the owner's slave. Indeed, the owners were free to "sell" their mozo servants to work on other finca, and many men found themselves thirty or forty miles away from home with no way to get out of the situation they had created for themselves. If they tried to escape, they were tracked down and whipped mercilessly. They were trapped, with no hope of ever working their way to freedom.

Cam updated Robby on Tiburcio's story, and they both agreed that the Christian message was the only way to free the Indians from debt and dependence on alcohol. It had worked for Tiburcio, and Cam was eager to share the same message with others.

That night Cam slept in a real bed for the first time in weeks. He was asleep almost as soon as his head touched the fluffy white pillow. He slept soundly, so soundly, in fact, that it nearly cost him his life.

"Cam, wake up!" Robby screamed in his ear.

Cam opened his eyes and looked around. It was dark, but he could feel Robby grasping his shoulders and shaking him vigorously. "What's up?" he stammered, still trying to get his bearings.

"An earthquake," shot back Robby over the sound of a loud crash. "I escaped outside, but I couldn't see you anywhere. How can you sleep through this? We have to get out of here now!"

Cam was suddenly wide awake. He threw back his sheet and headed for the door. Within seconds, he and Robby were standing in the street outside the mission house.

"Look at that!" exclaimed Robby, grabbing Cam and turning him around.

In the moonlight Cam watched with a mixture of horror and fascination. About half a mile down the street the cobblestone pavement was buckling in huge waves that were surging towards them.

"It looks just like the waves at Long Beach," blurted Cam, unable to take his eyes off the approaching undulations that raised and then dashed to pieces most of the buildings in their path.

The noise all around was horrendous. By now the nurses at the Presbyterian hospital directly across the street were rushing outside, pushing patients in wheelchairs and carrying others on stretchers. The two missionaries braced themselves as the rolling wave approached. The wave lifted them up and deposited them, a little dazed but unhurt, hard on the ground. They both scrambled to their feet.

"Let's help the nurses," suggested Cam, running across the crumbled street towards the hospital, which was miraculously still standing.

For the rest of the night and on into the morning, Cam and Robby ferried patients out of the hospital and helped make them as comfortable as possible in the middle of the street. Everyone in the city was camped out-of-doors. Most of the houses lay in rubble, and those that were still standing were too damaged to go back inside. Besides, nobody wanted to be inside if an aftershock occurred.

It was not until daybreak Christmas day that the full extent of the disaster was apparent. The crumbled remains of collapsed buildings littered the streets, and it seemed as though fires raged uncontrollably on each block.

By midmorning, city officials had set up their offices in the middle of the town square. Cam retrieved a dozen Bibles from the badly damaged mission house and walked to the town square to see whether there was anything he could do to help. As he made his way there, he spotted a man sitting in the gutter drinking whiskey. Cam wondered how many other people would be tempted to sit and drink their troubles away as the day went on. By the time he got to see the mayor in the town square, Cam had a plan. "Sir," he began, "I would like to present you with a Bible at this very difficult time."

"Thank you," replied the mayor, barely looking up.

Cam took a deep breath and spoke again. "I know you're an extremely busy man right now," he said, "but I wonder if you have considered what might happen if many of your citizens get drunk today. Surely you would agree there is enough chaos already. I urge you to order that no liquor be sold in the city until the situation is under control."

The mayor looked up and stared at Cam. Cam felt himself turning red. He wondered what the mayor was thinking about the scrawny, twenty-one-year-old American standing in front of him telling him what to do.

After a few moments of deliberation, the mayor turned to an official and barked, "Order a ban on liquor sales effective immediately."

"Yes, sir," responded the official, hurrying off to carry out the order.

Cam could hardly believe the mayor had taken his advice—or that he'd actually had the courage to give it in the first place. His time in Guatemala had certainly given him courage and confidence.

Christmas Day came and went in a blur of pulling screaming people from the rubble, helping dazed children find their parents, and setting up a makeshift tent village to serve as a hospital. It was forty-two hours from the time Cam had been roughly awakened in the middle of the earthquake until he was able to get more sleep. Exhausted, he collapsed onto the hard ground beside Robby in a makeshift tent and went straight to sleep. He didn't even bother to take off his boots.

The aftershocks continued for a month, with the worst one occurring on January 24, 1918. This quake managed to collapse those buildings that had survived the first jolt. Almost all of Guatemala City was leveled by the earthquake and its aftershocks. Many hundreds of people were killed, and funerals continued for days.

Cam did what he could to help with the aftermath of the disaster, but he was eager to get back on the trail selling Bibles again. Once enough relief workers were in place to deal with the crisis, he felt it was time for him to leave the earthquake-ravaged city. Once again Francisco Díaz accompanied him on his travels. Together they embarked on an eleven-month tour that would take them through Guatemala, El Salvador, Honduras, and Nicaragua.

It would have been a grueling trip for anyone to make, but it was made even more grueling when both Cam and Francisco came down with influenza. They were both ill for days, but they recovered, unlike millions of people around the world who died from the epidemic in 1918.

The more time Cam spent with Francisco Díaz, the more he came to admire the man's intelligence and determination. Francisco picked up new ideas quickly, and he soaked up Cam's Bible teaching like a sponge. Cam knew the Ladinos thought the Indians were slow and stupid, but that was because the Indians always had to speak to them in Spanish, a foreign language to them. Cam became convinced that the answer was to teach the Indians to read and write their own language, but their languages were not written down. The people had no dictionaries, no beginning readers, no pamphlets on how to grow better crops or how to treat simple illnesses. They had nothing written in their language. No wonder they lived with such dark superstitions— they had no access to scientific knowledge.

The path out of superstition and into the twentieth century was clear to Cam. It involved writing a tribe's language down, providing reading material in that language, and translating the Bible into it so that people would have the opportunity to embrace its truth. Of course, the path was easy to map out. It was quite another thing to actually carry it out.

Cam and Francisco were traveling along a jungle trail near the Nicaraguan border about nine months into their challenging trip when they sat down one evening around a smoky campfire. They were roasting a monkey Francisco had been given at the last village. As they sat waiting for the monkey to cook, they talked.

"Why doesn't someone start schools for Indian children?" asked Cam.

"Who do you have in mind, don Guillermo?" asked Francisco Díaz. "The Ladinos think it's beneath them to talk to an Indian, and the missionaries all learn Spanish and then spend their years trying to train the Indians to speak it, too."

"But surely there must be someone who could start schools to teach people in the local languages. What about a person like you? You can read and write," Cam suggested to Francisco.

"That is true," said Francisco, turning the stick the monkey was roasting on. "But what would be the point? I only know how to read Spanish. Most Indians work twelve hours a day. They don't have the time to learn a foreign language from the missionaries, much less from another Indian like me."

Cam sat staring at the fire for a long time. Someone needed to teach the Indians to read and write in their own language, but who?

Francisco Díaz interrupted his thoughts. "And what about you, don Guillermo? Why don't you stay and start a school for the Cakchiquel people? You could translate the Bible for us and teach us how to read it."

Cam glanced at his companion to see whether he was really serious. Francisco certainly looked it. "I don't think so," Cam finally spluttered, thinking of how impossible it would be. He hadn't even finished college yet, he'd never taken a course in language translation, Cakchiquel was one of the weirdest languages he'd ever heard, and once he stopped selling Bibles, he would have no income.

Cam wanted to tell Francisco it would be impossible for him to stay and do what he had suggested, but something inside him rebelled against the word *impossible*. Was it impossible to learn another language? Was it impossible to translate the Bible into that language? Was it impossible to start a school to teach Indians in that language? Was it impossible to find the money to live in Guatemala for a few more years?

With a sudden burst of clarity, Cam knew nothing was impossible with God. Not only were all these things possible, but he, William Cameron Townsend, was going to stay and do them!

The Logic of Language

By Christmas 1918, Cam was back in Guatemala City. He had hoped to meet up with Robby again, but Robby had been drafted into the army and had returned to the United States shortly before the war in Europe ended in November.

In Guatemala City, Cam stayed with a Presbyterian missionary couple. As he walked about the city, he was impressed by the rebuilding effort going on all around. When Cam had left Guatemala City eleven months before, it was nothing but a pile of rubble. Now the rubble was gone, and new buildings were sprouting up everywhere. Within a few more months, he figured, there would be virtually no sign left of the devastating earthquake that had leveled the city the previous Christmas.

While he was thankful for the hospitality of the missionary couple, Cam found it lonely without Robby around to talk to and share his experiences with. That is, until he met a single missionary woman from Chicago. Elvira Malmstrom was twenty-six years old, four years older than Cam. The two of them liked each other right away. Elvira spoke perfect Spanish, and she laughed at all Cam's jokes. She played the organ for the Christmas carol singing and helped Cam organize his letter writing so he didn't miss anyone. Indeed, Cam soon found himself relying on Elvira more and more. She liked working with children and was as eager to get out into the Indian villages as he was. Cam invited Elvira to visit him in San Antonio, where he was headed after Christmas.

In February, Elvira and the Treichlers, a couple working with Central American Mission, arrived in San Antonio to visit. Cam was not as far along in his efforts to set up a school as he would have liked since he had suffered a bout of malaria and was still not feeling well. However, he was glad to show the three missionaries around San Antonio.

As the visit progressed, Cam was delighted to see that Elvira fitted in easily among the Indians. Elvira visited the sick and even learned a few Cakchiquel phrases. By the time she was scheduled to return to Guatemala City, Cam had come to a conclusion: Elvira would make a wonderful wife. He proposed to her on Valentine's Day 1919, and two days later she said yes.

Now that Cam was going to be a married man, Mr. Treichler took him aside and asked him how he planned to support a wife. Cam wasn't too sure, but Mr. Treichler had a solution. Since Cam had stopped selling Bibles, he suggested that Cam join Central American Mission. Such a move would allow Cam to keep working among the Cakchiquel Indians and provide a network through which he could raise the needed monthly support.

Cam and Elvira talked things over and decided that joining Central American Mission would be the wisest thing to do. Their names were submitted to the mission's board, and in March, four months before they were to be married, Cam and Elvira were officially accepted as CAM missionaries.

The wedding took place on July 9, 1919, Cam's twenty-third birthday. Cam had wanted to marry on his birthday, just as his father had married on his birthday. Many friends helped make it a special day. Mr. Treichler gave Cam a gold coin that a jeweler crafted into a ring for Elvira. The president of CAM bought Cam a three-piece suit to replace the tattered clothes he wore on his travels around Central America, and a Ladino Christian woman made Elvira a spectacular wedding dress. None of Cam's family was able to make it to the wedding, but Elvira's brother Carl, a pastor in Chicago, arrived in time to be best man.

The honeymoon was not a typical one. Cam and his new bride wanted to show Carl as much of the work in Guatemala as possible. The day after the wedding, the three of them set out on an eighty-five-mile trek to visit as many Cakchiquel Indians as possible. An Indian porter went with them, carrying Elvira's portable organ, while the two men carried the trio's clothing and other supplies. Elvira rode Pilgrim, Cam's newly acquired donkey. When the group came to a village, they would set up Elvira's organ and hold a service and hand out Bible tracts.

Two weeks later, Carl Malmstrom returned to the United States. It was time for Cam and Elvira to make a home together. They decided to settle in Antigua for the first few months and make regular visits to San Antonio to oversee the school Cam had set up. It was the first school for Indians in all of Central America. Overseeing the school from afar proved impractical, however, and when they received a gift of seventy dollars from Moody Church in Chicago, Cam and Elvira used it to build their own single-room cornstalk house in San Antonio.

The couple had plenty of work to do once they settled in. Elvira played her organ at all the church meetings and taught sewing, singing, and organ playing. She also visited the sick. In many ways she was a perfect wife, except for one thing, which Cam was unaware of until after the wedding. Elvira had an awful temper. But it was no ordinary bad temper. Sometimes she would become enraged for no apparent reason and would rant and rave and throw things around. In the meantime, Cam was left to ponder what the problem could be. At first

Elvira's behavior scared him a great deal, but over time he came to accept that she suffered from some kind of mental illness. As a result, regardless of how she behaved towards him, Cam decided he would always try to be kind and helpful to her.

Cam was delighted to have Francisco Díaz working alongside him again. His goal had always been to work himself out of a job, and he felt that Francisco was the perfect man to take over running the school. Francisco was a conscientious man who was well respected by the members of the local church. Much to Cam's dismay, though, Francisco Díaz came down with malaria and died a few days later. It was a devastating blow to Cam, but he became more determined than ever to fulfill Francisco's challenge to him and translate the New Testament into the Cakchiquel language.

The work was painfully slow. First Cam had to develop an ear for the language so that he could imitate its sounds. The language was not at all like English; so many words sounded the same but had very different meanings. The Cakchiquel words for red, stingy, black, and flea all sounded the same except for subtle differences in the "k" sound at the end of each word. The first word had an English-sounding k. The second word had a k that was made while coughing, while the third word had a little popping sound after the k. In the fourth word, the k was a kind of choking sound that could be made only when the Adam's apple was at the bottom of the throat. Cam, who'd had no training in writing down a language, was baffled as to how to record these four different "k" sounds.

Recording the sounds, though, was not his worst problem. In English, most verbs like "skip" or "play" or "eat" have a certain number of forms, or beginnings and endings that can be added to change their meaning a little. Skip can become skipping, play can become replayed, or eat can become eaten. Adding "ed" to a verb puts the action into the past tense, adding "ing" means the action is happening in the present, and adding "re" at the beginning means to repeat the action. But when Cam came to the use of verbs in the Cakchiquel language, he could find no pattern at all. The verbs were all very long words, and he could not understand how they possibly made sense. He wrote page after page of notes and listened to Cakchiquel Indians speaking for days, but the verbs remained a mystery to him. The more he tried to understand the verb forms, the more stuck he seemed to become. He needed help if he was to be successful in his translation efforts.

One day while Cam was in Antigua buying supplies he heard a man speaking in English. He hurried over to introduce himself and discovered the man was the well-known American archaeologist Dr. Gates. Dr. Gates was as happy to see a fellow American as Cam was to see him. The two of them sat down together at a nearby cafe. Over coffee they had an interesting conversation. Dr. Gates told Cam all about his efforts to locate ancient manuscripts in the area, and Cam told Dr. Gates about his frustration deciphering the Cakchiquel language. "It's the verbs," Cam said. "I can't find any patterns in the verbs. I know if I could, that would help me unlock the language."

Dr. Gates rubbed his chin thoughtfully. "I'm not very familiar with the Cakchiquel language, but I'd have a good guess at where you are going wrong," he began. "I suspect you're starting with the way we speak English and other languages that come from Latin and you are trying to fit Cakchiquel into that pattern. I have heard Dr. Sapir, the linguist at the University of Chicago, speak, and he suggests doing just the opposite in a situation like yours. Forget about the English way of putting words together and comparing Cakchiquel words to English words. Instead, start learning the most basic Cakchiquel words until you become familiar with them and begin to see the unique pattern within the Cakchiquel language."

"Of course, that makes perfect sense!" exclaimed Cam. "Every language has its own pattern of usage, and I will find that pattern much faster if I stop trying to compare Cakchiquel to English."

"Exactly," said Dr. Gates, clapping Cam on the shoulder. "I'm sure you will find the language has its own logic."

Cam's excitement was growing by the minute. "I don't know why I couldn't see it before. It's like the number system. It took me a long time to work it out. But once I did, the logic was plain and simple.

The Cakchiquel Indians counted one, two, three, four, five, six, seven, eight, nine, like we would, but when they got to ten, it was 'one man,' and then one man one, one man two, one man three, and so on up to twenty, which they called two men."

Cam took a sip of his hot, sweet coffee before continuing. "I couldn't imagine why ten would be one man and twenty would be two men, until an Indian boy showed me. One man has ten fingers, two men have twenty fingers, and so on. It was as simple as that. I was so used to our number system that at first I didn't see the inner logic of the Cakchiquel system."

Dr. Gates laughed. "Tell me more about your work in San Antonio. It sounds very interesting."

Later in the afternoon, after the two men had parted company, Cam could hardly wait to get back to San Antonio. Thanks to a chance meeting with an American archaeologist, he knew he now had an important key to use in unlocking the Cakchiquel language. As he led his donkey, laden with supplies, Cam thought about how much faster the process of deciphering the language would be if he just knew more about language acquisition and translation. What other suggestions could someone with the knowledge of Dr. Sapir give him?

The next day he went straight to work taking more notes and listening to the Indians chatter to each other. Within days, Cam began to see how the language worked. It was no wonder he could not work out the verb forms—there were thousands of them. A single verb like "walk" could have up to one hundred thousand different beginnings and endings that added to or changed its meaning. Many of these beginnings and endings could be bundled up together, making extremely long and complicated words. Things could also be added to "walk" to tell the listener who was walking, where they were walking, in what direction they were walking—how many they were walking with, how fast they were walking, at what time they were walking, and the list could go on and on. And all of this could be found in a single word!

Within a few months, Cam had a basic grasp of the Cakchiquel language. However, before he could begin translating, he had to devise a method for writing the language. He decided to use the Spanish alphabet, using one letter to stand for a particular Cakchiquel sound. This way he could build complex Cakchiquel words using only four or five letters.

Once he had an alphabet, Cam was ready to begin his translation work. He chose to start translating the Gospel of Mark. Although he knew he would make many mistakes, he hoped his translation would make enough sense to tell the Cakchiquel Indians about God. An Indian man from the nearby village of Comalapa helped him with the task.

Elvira helped, too. After Cam was satisfied with his translation of a passage, she typed up the manuscript. Finally, when Cam was satisfied he had a good "temporary" draft of the first four chapters of Mark, he took them to Antigua to have them printed.

It was not an easy task finding a printer, but eventually Cam tracked one down in the mayor's office. Cam was standing in the office talking to the printer about some of the punctuation marks when the mayor walked in. "What's going on?" the mayor asked, surveying the pile of papers in Cam's hand.

"I've been translating the Gospel of Mark into Cakchiquel, and now I have the first four chapters ready for printing," Cam answered with a touch of pride.

The mayor frowned. "What a waste of time!" he exploded. "We're trying to civilize the Indians and teach them Spanish ways, and you want them to learn to read in their own backward language. Don't you understand, we are trying to get rid of these languages for good."

Cam gulped nervously. What should he say? One wrong word and the printer would be forbidden to print the precious pages. He prayed a quick prayer for inspiration. A moment later he had it. "But mayor," he said respectfully, "look how it is written." He held a page up for the mayor to see. "There is Cakchiquel on one side of the page, but the other side is written in Spanish. This way the Indians can learn to read in their own language and in Spanish all in one book."

The mayor studied the page. "Hum. I suppose it will be all right then. You can print it," he said to the printer as he strolled out of the office.

Cam let out a sigh of relief. The printer took some more notes on what Cam wanted done and promised to have the printed pages ready within a month. He even gave Cam a discount, since the mayor had now approved the project.

A month later the first batch of pamphlets containing the four chapters of the Gospel of Mark were ready, and Cam walked into town to pick them up. He had expected the Christians in San Antonio to be excited when they finally saw the printed pages, but nowhere near as excited as they turned out to be. "See, God speaks our language." They laughed and cried at the same time as they handed the pamphlets from person to person.

Soon all the copies of the pamphlet were sold. Many of the local Indian preachers, who could not read a word, carried the Bible portion with them wherever they went. Soon adults from the surrounding Cakchiquel villages were knocking on the Townsends' door asking when Cam was going to start teaching reading so they could learn to read the Bible passages for themselves.

Chapter 8

Promise and Loss

It was November 1920, and Antigua was abuzz with news of the Central American Congress. The congress was a historic meeting of politicians and diplomats from all the countries of Central America who had gathered to explore the possibility of uniting into one large country.

Cam, like everyone else, knew about the gathering, but he hadn't given it much thought until a woman came to him with a suggestion. "They are having a Catholic mass in honor of this congress. Why don't you organize a Protestant service for it?" the woman said.

"What would be the point?" Cam asked, but even as he spoke, an idea came flooding into his head. There could be a lot of point! He could use such a service to showcase the work among the Cakchiquel Indians, especially the way they were learning to read and write in their own language. What better way to introduce the top officials of all the countries of Central America to the idea of translating the Bible into native languages.

Cam went straight to work. He and Elvira sent official-looking invitations to every dignitary attending the congress and then prayed they would come to the service. Elvira also got together a group of San Antonio Christians who practiced singing some Cakchiquel hymns she had translated.

Finally, Friday afternoon arrived, and Cam was relieved to see the pews in the small Protestant church filling up fast. The service went without a hitch, and when it was over, Cam thanked everyone for attending. He wasn't sure exactly who was there, but most of the people looked important and had arrived in diplomatic cars. After Cam had finished his short speech, a tall, distinguished man rose to his feet. The church became silent. "I would like to say a few words on behalf of the congressmen from Guatemala," he said.

Cam wasn't sure what the man was about to say, but he had no choice but to let him speak. The congressman walked forward. He shook Cam's hand vigorously and cleared his throat. "It is truly marvelous to see what the Bible has done for these Indians—Indians whom the Spanish people thought were nothing but animals and used for generations as beasts of burden. I commend you on your work."

With that the man sat down. As he did so, another man sprang to his feet. He introduced himself as the brother of the president of Honduras. "I too am delighted to see what has been done for these Indians. I commend your work," he said.

When this man sat down, the secretary of the Central American Congress stood and complimented Cam and the Indians on running a fine church service.

It was all more than Cam had hoped for. Indeed, the service had been an eye-opener for him. Although it had not been a part of the official congress, Cam had nonetheless invited many important men from around the region, and they had willingly come. As a result, a seed had been planted in each of them that Indians could learn to read and write in their own language and that it was possible to translate the Bible into the various Indian languages.

Cam and the Cakchiquel Indians prayed earnestly that the seed would grow in these important Central American leaders and that one day every tribe in the region would have the Bible in its own tongue.

Early the following month—December—Robby Robinson returned to Guatemala. He had survived the last days of the war in Europe unscathed and arrived in the country with his new bride, Genevieve. Cam was delighted to see his old friend again and know that Robby hadn't turned his back on the work they had embarked on together among the Indians. The two of them had a lot of catching up to do, along with planning for the future. Their first joint venture was to organize the Cakchiquel Bible Conference Cam had scheduled for January 1921.

Cam eagerly shared with Robby that an evangelist from the United States had agreed to be the guest speaker at the conference. Leonard Legters had been a missionary to the Comanche Indians in Oklahoma for many years. Although Cam had never heard him speak, a friend from college had recommended him as a "lively" preacher.

Once Leonard Legters arrived for the conference, Cam decided the word *lively* was an understatement! L.L., as everyone called Leonard Legters, was a fireball of activity. He preached day and night, using anything he could get his hands on to illustrate his sermons. The only thing he complained about was having to stand still while his words were translated first into Spanish by Cam and then into Cakchiquel from the Spanish. L.L. quickly came to appreciate the idea of reading and preaching directly in the Cakchiquel language.

The Cakchiquel Indians flocked to the Bible conference. As word got around about L.L., more and more people kept showing up for the services. Even better than the large crowd in attendance, by week's end there were sixty new Christian converts in the area, including one of the tribal chiefs.

When the conference was over, Robby and Genevieve Robinson packed up their few belongings and headed northwest for Panajachel, a picturesque town situated on the northern edge of Lake Atitlan. Cam, Elvira, L.L., and an Indian translator set off in the opposite direction over the mountains by mule. L.L. was eager to preach in as many Indian villages as possible before returning to the United States.

By the time their speaking trek through the mountains was over, Cam was sure he had made a friend for life. L.L. promised to return the following year for another conference and to promote the needs of the Guatemalan Indians when he got back to the United States. True to his word, each letter that L.L. wrote to Cam contained an article or letter he had written to some Christian newspaper or magazine about the needs and challenges he had seen firsthand in Guatemala.

In the meantime, the trip through the mountains had proved too much for Elvira. Several times along the way she had gone into uncontrollable outbursts of rage, screaming for the police to come to her aid over nothing. After the trip, Cam decided the best thing he could do for his wife was to send her home for a break. She could stay with her parents and get some rest. Cam promised to join her as soon as he could.

Before Cam left, Robby agreed to take over administering the school and oversee the Bible training work for pastors Cam had begun the year before. In 1921, four years after arriving in Guatemala, Cam was able to join Elvira in America. He arrived back in Los Angeles, glad to see his sisters again and catch up on their brood of children. His brother Paul had just married, and Cam was delighted to learn that his new sister-in-law, Laura, was very interested in becoming a missionary.

Elvira had enjoyed the time with her parents, but her mental state seemed to be no better. Sometimes she was wonderful company, while at other times she would become uncontrollably angry. Cam took her to a psychiatrist to find out whether there was anything that could be done for her and, if not, whether she should even go back to Guatemala.

The psychiatrist could offer no help. There was little in the way of drugs available at the time to treat someone with Elvira's condition. However, the doctor did encourage Cam to take Elvira back to the mission field if she wanted to go. He explained that where Elvira lived had little to do with her outbursts of rage.

After the visit to the psychiatrist, Cam felt confident he should return to the mission field, but first he had a few things to take care of. He decided to join the Church of the Open Door in Los Angeles, since it had a strong interest in missions. There he met a young couple, Dr. and Mrs. Ainslie, who had been thinking of becoming missionaries. After hearing Cam speak, the Ainslies became convinced they should sign up for Guatemala. Paul and Laura Townsend also decided to join Cam in Guatemala.

While at home, Cam visited many old friends. One was Mrs. Heim, his fifth-grade Sunday school teacher. Mrs. Heim listened attentively as Cam described his plans for the Cakchiquel Indians. Cam wanted to build a proper school for them, as well as a home for abandoned children. He also wanted to set up a medical clinic and install a power generator so the Indians could have lights in their homes. Mrs. Heim, like everyone else, was impressed with the plan. She just had one question: "How are you going to pay for it all, since you don't have much financial support?"

Cam had thought about this too, but it didn't worry him. He assured Mrs. Heim that if it was God's work done in God's way, He would supply all of their needs. Mrs. Heim nodded in agreement; her Sunday school student had learned his lessons well.

Cam also visited with Charles Fuller, who ran a very large Bible class in the area. Mr. Fuller was very impressed with Cam's account of how the Indian pastors were being trained in all aspects of missionary work. He and his family volunteered to support two Cakchiquel pastors. Cam was overwhelmed. His dreams for the Cakchiquel Indians were becoming a reality right before his eyes.

Soon after meeting with Charles Fuller, Cam met a man who donated a printing press in good condition to the mission. Just as Cam was wondering how he would pay to transport the printing press to Guatemala, he received a letter from Mrs. Heim. The letter contained a check for three thousand dollars. Cam sat and stared at the check for several minutes. Tears welled in his eyes. Now he could pay to have the printing press shipped to Antigua and still have money left over for several other things.

It was with grateful hearts that Cam and Elvira Townsend left the United States to return to their cornstalk hut in San Antonio in February 1922. Elvira was no better, but she was no worse either, and Cam felt he had done everything he could to help her with her condition. Elvira was willing to return, and Cam was happy to have her with him.

Robby and Genevieve Robinson had done a wonderful job of keeping the mission going while the Townsends were away. Indeed, Robby seemed to have found his niche working with the Indian pastors, so Cam suggested he take over that side of the work. This would free Cam up to keep on with his Bible translation.

Things were working out well. Four months after his return, Cam decided to get together with Robby to plan the next Cakchiquel Bible conference. Since his wife was away for ten days, Robby decided they should meet at his home on Lake Atitlan. Cam looked forward to the opportunity to spend several days with his old friend.

Robby met Cam in Guatalon on the southern side of the lake. The two of them made their way slowly around the shore. Along the way they stopped to hand out tracts and sell the pamphlet containing the chapters of Mark's gospel translated into Cakchiquel.

The two men arrived at Robby's house on June 23, 1922. As they walked up the trail that led to the front entrance, a man with a sack slung over his shoulder made his way over to them. "Ah, don

Robby," the man began. "I was just coming to find you. I have a gift for you. It is nothing compared to what you have done for us, but it is the best I have."

With that, the man heaved the sack from his shoulder. Cam caught the unmistakable aroma of fresh coffee beans.

Robby smiled. "Thank you, don Pedro. Praise God everything worked out okay," he said.

When Pedro departed, Robby told Cam the story. Pedro's wife had had a serious case of gangrene poisoning. A doctor had passed through town and had told Pedro there was no hope for his wife and she was surely bound to die. Seeing how desperately ill she was, Pedro prepared his wife's funeral; he even readied a crypt for her body.

Robby, however, believed that God could heal the woman, and he began to encourage Pedro to pray with him. He visited the woman and sat through the night with her. He sang hymns to her and soaked her infected feet in warm water. By morning, the gangrene was receding, and slowly the woman began to recover. Within a week she was well again.

Cam was heartened by the story. "If we will do the possible, God will do the impossible," he said.

After lunch Robby suggested they go for a swim. It was a still, clear afternoon, and there was hardly a ripple on the surface of the lake. Soon both men were splashing about in the cool, fresh water. They swam out several hundred yards and floated on their backs. As he floated, Cam looked up at the clear, blue sky. He hadn't felt so relaxed in months.

It was good to be back with his old friend, and the Bible conference they were planning was going to be an exciting event.

About halfway to shore, Cam looked back to see how closely Robby was following. He could hardly believe what he saw. Robby was about one hundred yards behind him, but he wasn't floating along leisurely as he had been. Instead Robby's arms were flailing, and his head was shaking wildly. Cam swam toward his friend at full speed, thinking of the time he had nearly drowned in the canal in Fresno, California. "Don't let this happen to Robby. There's so much work to be done," he prayed under his breath as he swam.

Within seconds Cam had his forearm locked around his friend's neck. But Robby was much heavier than he and slipped under the water. Cam stayed with him, struggling to resurface, but instead was pulled down deeper. About nine feet down, Robby went limp. Cam dragged him to the surface. As Cam gasped several deep breaths of air, Robby's body slipped under the water again. Cam knew he did not have the strength to pull him up, so instead he swam ashore as fast as he could and called for help.

Several fishermen launched their boats and rowed to the spot where Robby had gone under. Cam could see Robby's motionless body at the bottom of the clear lake. Two of the fishermen dived into the water to retrieve Robby. As soon as Robby was pulled into the boat, Cam began mouth-to-mouth resuscitation. He kept it up while Robby's body was carried off the boat and onto the shore. Indeed, he kept it up for as long as he could. But two hours after first seeing Robby go under the water, Cam finally gave up the struggle. He had to face it. William Elbert Robinson, his loyal friend from Occidental College and fellow missionary to the Cakchiquel Indians, was dead.

Cam dreaded sending a telegram to Genevieve, Robby's wife. The couple had been married for less than three years, and Robby's death was impossible to explain. Robby was a strong swimmer, and it had been a calm day on the lake.

Three days later, on Tuesday morning, June 27, 1922, the funeral service was held. Genevieve had made it home late the night before. She was as stunned as everyone else was by Robby's death. The mayor of Panajachel declared it a day of mourning, and the service was held in the school, the only building large enough for the enormous crowd that gathered for the funeral.

Ironically, Robby was buried in the crypt that had been prepared for Pedro's wife who had made the miraculous recovery from gangrene. On Robby's gravestone were inscribed the words, "W. E. Robinson, Bearer of Good News."

As Cam stood beside the grave of his friend, he felt more alone than he ever had before. There was so much work to do, and the two men who had helped him the most, Francisco Díaz and Elbert "Robby" Robinson, had both died unexpectedly.

Chapter 9

A Job Completed

Six months after Robby's funeral, Cam was attending the Bible conference he had been planning with Robby on the day of his drowning. It had been difficult adjusting to life without his old friend around, but there had been a lot to keep Cam's mind busy. Cam's brother Paul and sister-in-law Laura had come to help with the mission work. Paul was as practical and hands-on as ever and immediately took charge of supervising construction of the new buildings the mission was erecting in San Antonio. Mrs. Heim had sent Cam another generous donation, this time four thousand dollars, which he had used to buy building materials. Paul and a crew of Indian men set to work building a proper boarding school. Soon one hundred children from outlying areas were living in the new facility, supervised by three American women missionaries. The children had been sent to the school by their parents to learn to read and write the Cakchiquel language. A medical clinic was also built in the town, and Central American Mission provided a nurse to oversee it. Dr. Ainslie, whom Cam had met while in Los Angeles on furlough, now worked at the Presbyterian hospital in Guatemala City and was on call to handle difficult cases at the clinic.

Paul was a fast worker, and once the school and clinic were built, he began work on an orphanage. Until it was completed, Cam arranged for the needy children to stay with various Christians around the village. He and Elvira took in two such children themselves, Elena Trejo and Joe Chicol. Both were eager students, and the Townsends had high hopes that one day they would carry on the work among the Cakchiquel Indians in the area.

Cam had more plans, too—big plans. He confided in Paul that he wanted San Antonio to become a model Indian town, an example of how, with a little encouragement, Indians could learn to stand on their own two feet. In response to this, a coffee manufacturing company in St. Louis, whose manager had read about Cam in a Christian magazine, sent him a turbine and coffee bean sheller. The equipment allowed the Indians to shell their own coffee beans and so derive more profit for themselves by not having to pay a Ladino to do it.

All this was heartening to Cam, but none of it was as exciting as the arrival of Archer Anderson in February 1923. Archer had just graduated from the Philadelphia School of the Bible, where in an edition of the Central American Mission magazine *Bulletin* he had read about the work Robby was doing at the time of his death. As a result, Archer decided to come to Guatemala and continue from where Robby had left off.

Archer Anderson turned out to be quite a whirlwind. Cam was amazed at how quickly he adjusted to the Cakchiquel way of life. Within six weeks of his arrival, Archer had fixed up the building Robby had bought to serve as a Bible school. In no time at all, the Robinson Bible Institute, named in honor of Robby, was up and running. Fifteen students from three surrounding villages were enrolled in the school.

The Townsends went to stay in Robby's old house so that Cam could serve as translator for Archer Anderson when he taught class. However, Cam could see he wouldn't be needed for long. Archer was picking up the Cakchiquel language at an amazing pace. Indeed, he was soon fluent in the language and had no need for Cam to be his translator.

By the end of 1923, everything was going well for Cameron Townsend and the group of missionaries who worked with him. Indeed, things were going so well it actually created problems for Cam. Other missionaries began complaining about Cam's work among the Cakchiquel Indians. Whatever Cam did, someone would criticize it. He would invite Indians into his home and was criticized for being too informal. He was criticized because he spoke to the Indians in Cakchiquel instead of requiring them to learn Spanish, when everyone knew that Cakchiquel was a dead-end language. He was criticized because he had no formal Bible training and yet he ran a Bible institute. He was also criticized for treating the Indians as a separate group of people from the Ladinos. By doing so, people said he was encouraging competition between the two groups. The list of things people complained about went on and on.

Finally, Central American Mission sent Dr. Lewis Sperry Chafer, the mission's executive secretary, from his office in Dallas, Texas, to Guatemala to investigate the work Cam was doing and the complaints against him. Cam had recently broken his ankle and was hobbling around when Dr. Chafer arrived. Despite his injury, he borrowed Paul's Model T Ford and spent the next fourteen days driving Dr. Chafer around the Indian villages in the area and then down the rutted, muddy roads through the Guatemalan countryside and across the border into El Salvador. As they drove, Dr. Chafer grilled Cam on every aspect of his mission work. His main concern was why Cam felt it more important to do translation work than "normal" missionary work.

By the time the tour was over, Dr. Chafer was convinced that the Indians had a right to read the

Bible in their own language and that translating the Bible into a local language was a worthwhile activity for a missionary to undertake. This was good news to Cam, but there was some bad news, too. Dr. Chafer was only one of eight men who would have to vote on the issue of Bible translation at the 1925 council meeting of Central American Mission, which was to be held in Chicago. Cam groaned. He knew he would have to go to Chicago to meet the other seven members of the council, even though it meant taking precious time out from his translation work.

In 1925, the Townsends visited California again and then traveled on to Chicago. The Central American Mission council meeting was held at Moody Church, Elvira's home church. Cam met with the council members in the morning and answered their questions. Then, during lunch break, he walked along North Avenue with Mr. Smith, the man on the council who seemed the most opposed to the idea of Central American Mission's supporting Bible translation. By now Cam was very frustrated with the whole situation. Even though Dr. Chafer had given a stirring speech commending the work Cam was doing in Guatemala, Mr. Smith was not convinced.

Cam tried to talk to him some more about his work in Guatemala, but Mr. Smith would not listen. Finally, in a rare show of temper, Cam snapped, "It doesn't matter whether you like it or not, Mr. Smith, the Cakchiquel New Testament is going to be translated!" With that he turned and walked briskly back to the church alone.

Later that afternoon, a vote was taken as to whether Cam should be allowed to continue his work. Six men voted for him to continue, and two, including Mr. Smith, voted for him to stop his Bible translation and do routine missionary work.

Six to two was enough to win the vote, and Cam felt very pleased with the result. Now, he told himself, nothing could keep him from his translating work. He was eager to get back to Guatemala and continue. However, while he was away, Paul and Laura Townsend had found a new calling. Paul had been offered a job teaching at Presbyterian Industrial College in Guatemala City. While Cam was delighted to see his brother using his talents to teach others, Paul had left quite a gap to fill, and Cam found himself busier than ever.

A year after he returned to Guatemala from Chicago, Cam counted up the number of days he had been able to spend working on translating the New Testament into Cakchiquel. It added up to a paltry twelve days. As Cam thought about it, he remembered the conversation he'd had with Mr. Smith. He had been rude to Mr. Smith, and even though he had won the vote, his Bible translation was at a virtual standstill. As he thought about it, Cam decided it was time to apologize for his behavior. He took out a sheet of paper and wrote, "Dear Mr. Smith, Please forgive my anger. I've found that unless the Lord undertakes, I will never finish the work of the Cakchiquel translation."

Cam felt much better after he had mailed the letter. He seemed to have more energy, too. Suddenly his translation work began to fall into place. By 1926, he had completed writing a forty-nine page grammar of the Cakchiquel language. He sent a copy of the grammar to Dr. Sapir at the University of Chicago for his comments. Dr. Sapir wrote back an encouraging letter. Cam breathed a sigh of relief. While he thought he was on the right track in his understanding of the Cakchiquel language, it was very encouraging to have such a noted linguist as Dr. Sapir endorse his work.

Cam kept busy at translating the New Testament, despite the fact that other things constantly vied for his attention: A race had to be built to carry water from the river to the turbine to run the coffee sheller, a chief became ill and had to be accompanied to the hospital in Guatemala City, and pastors needed to be trained. By the spring of 1928, Cam was close to finishing translating the New Testament, although he didn't seem to be able to find the time he needed for one last push to finish the project. In desperation, he hit on a new plan. He and Elvira would leave Guatemala and all its distractions and finish the translation work at his parents' home in California. He took two Cakchiquel speakers—his foster son Joe Chicol and Trinidad Bac, a local preacher—with him to the United States.

The plan worked flawlessly. With no interruptions, Cam and his two helpers were able to finish translating the New Testament and double-check their work. Finally, on October 15, 1928, the massive job was complete.

Always ready to hold some kind of service or cel-ebration, Cam invited his friends and relatives to a Thanksgiving service before the manuscript was sent away for typesetting and printing. At the service he invited his parents to the front, where he had them write in the last two words of the book of Revelation. Cam thanked everyone for supporting him through the ten long years it had taken to translate the New Testament into Cakchiquel. He also told them stories of how the small portions of Scripture that had already been printed and distributed had changed many lives in San Antonio and how the Cakchiquel Indians who had seen the pamphlets marveled that God also spoke their language.

It was a wonderful evening. The following morn-ing Cam wrapped the pages of the New Testament in brown paper, tied them with string, and mailed them off to the American Bible Society in New York, where the type would be set. After the typesetting was done, a set of page proofs would be sent back to Cam for him to double-check for accuracy. Cam had been told to expect the proofs in about six months.

While he waited, Cam was not a man to sit around doing nothing. He had enough ideas rolling around in his head to keep ten men busy, but in 1929 one idea seemed more important than all the others. Over his years in Guatemala, he had thought about reaching the hundreds of other Indian tribes in Central and South America with the gospel. Indeed, once work on translating the Bible into Cakchiquel was complete, Cam intended to move on to work among another tribe. Many of these tribes, like the Cakchiquel, lived within easy walking distance of trains or buses and other forms of transportation. They lived in areas that were well mapped and documented. However, there were other tribes who didn't live in such accessible areas. Cam had recently learned how most of the Amazon Basin's two and a half million square miles of land was mostly unmapped and unexplored. No one could say for sure how many tribal groups lived there, but it was estimated that over five hundred different languages were spoken by people living in the Amazon jungle.

One of the great hindrances to reaching these tribes with the gospel was how long it took to get in and out of the area. Indeed, there were only a handful of missionaries working in the Amazon Basin, and these missionaries reported that it could take a week of hard slog through the jungle just to cover ten miles. At that pace, missionaries on foot would never cover the millions of square miles that needed to be covered to make contact with all the tribes living there.

This may have seemed an insurmountable problem to some, but to Cameron Townsend it was a new challenge. There had to be some way to efficiently reach these people, and Cam intended to find it. As he thought about the situation, there seemed only one possible answer: airplanes. If missionaries could fly in and out of remote areas, the work of reaching the Amazonian Indian tribes with the gospel could be accomplished much faster.

Cam wrote to Major Dargue, a U.S. navy pilot he had met in Guatemala, and asked him to estimate what would be needed to begin a flying program over the Amazon Basin. Major Dargue's reply was thorough. In his opinion, flying missionaries in and out of the Amazon region would need a minimum of three amphibious airplanes, plus pilots, mechanics, radio operators, hangars for housing and repairing the airplanes, fuel tanks, spare parts, and insurance. All in all, Major Dargue estimated the cost for such an operation to be about forty-five thousand dollars a year.

At first Cam was very excited about it all. While forty-five thousand dollars was a lot of money, he was sure American Christians would see the need for getting missionaries in and out of remote areas quickly and safely. Cam may have been right, and the money may well have been raised, except for one thing: October 29, 1929. On that day—Black Tuesday as it came to be known—the decade of prosperity that followed World War I came to a screeching halt. The stock market crashed, causing many Americans to lose their jobs. The Great Depression that would stretch on through the 1930s had begun.

Everyone in the United States was affected in some way by the Depression. Many of those who didn't lose their jobs were forced to take massive pay cuts. Of course, churches soon began to feel the effects of the Depression, too. Offerings plunged, and missionaries were told not to expect financial support anymore. Indeed, many missionaries were called home by their sponsoring denomination or mission. It was Cam's worst nightmare. At a time when he wanted to ask Christians to stretch their budgets to support airplanes for missionaries, most people no longer had enough money to cover their own basic needs.

To make matters worse, a missionary whom Cam greatly respected visited him. When he heard that Cam was thinking of eventually leaving the Cakchiquel Indians and going to work among a tribe in the Amazon who needed to learn to read and write, he was appalled. "But you're just beginning to reach these people!" he exclaimed. "It would be like abandoning newborn babies; you give them the Bible and then you leave them. What would they think?"

Cam said nothing, and the missionary went on. "When you go to a new tribe, you become spiritually responsible for them," he lectured. "Think how long it would take another missionary to learn as much about the tribe as you know. Don't waste all you know by moving on to another language. Stay and work where God has put you."

When the missionary left, Cam told Elvira he didn't want any dinner. Instead, he went into the bedroom and shut the door behind him. His mind was in turmoil. What was he thinking! Here he wanted to ask American Christians to provide money for airplanes and pilots to push ahead his plan of reaching other Indian tribes in the region with the gospel when the Christians at home were having trouble buying food for their children. Perhaps his missionary visitor had been right.

Perhaps he should just stay working among the Cakchiquel Indians. After all, the school was expanding, the medical clinic was busy every day, and many Indians had become Christian converts.

Thinking about the problem didn't seem to help Cam. In fact, the more he thought about it, the more confused he became. In the end he decided on a desperate course of action, one he had never taken before. He prayed and asked God to show him through the Bible what to do. He then reached over, picked up his Bible, and flipped it open. He closed his eyes and pointed to a spot on the page. He opened his eyes again and began to read. His finger had fallen on Luke 15:4: "What man amongst you, having a hundred sheep, if he lose one of them, doth not leave the ninety and nine in the wilderness, and go after that which is lost, until he find it?"

Cam sat for a long time staring at the verse. One hundred sheep, ninety-nine of them safe in the fold and one lost, he thought. And the shepherd didn't stay in the safe place with the ninety-nine. Instead, he left the safe and secure place and went after a single lost sheep. Cam asked himself what this could mean for him. Was the verse indicating that he should leave the Cakchiquel Indians with the New Testament in their language and move on to look for another tribe who had not yet heard the gospel? And when he had given them the gospel in their language, did it mean he should move on to find another tribe, and then another after that? Cam felt that was what the verse was showing him, but he would have to think about it some more to make sure.

Chapter 10

The New Testament at Last

The more Cam thought about the verse from Luke, the more he believed that God was urging him to forge ahead with his plans. He decided that as soon as he and Elvira had read the proof sheets of the Cakchiquel New Testament they would find another tribe to work with. In the meantime, Cam thought more about the airplane project. As he did so, he met a man named Lynn Van Sickle, who could fly a little and who became interested in the idea of using airplanes to help missionaries do their jobs more effectively. Lynn Van Sickle had just graduated from Moody Bible Institute, and Cam urged him to join Central American Mission. Maybe one day, he told Lynn, CAM would have an air division of its own.

Finally the page proofs for the Cakchiquel New Testament arrived for checking. By now Trinidad Bac and Joe Chicol had returned to San Antonio, and Cam could settle down to weeks of scrutinizing every letter of every word. He knew that a single mistake could change the meaning of an entire passage and he wanted the translation to be as accurate as possible.

By November the job was complete, and Cam sent the manuscript to New York for printing and binding. It was time for him and Elvira to head back to Guatemala. On the way back to Guatemala, Cam decided to visit the Central American Mission leaders at their headquarters in Dallas, Texas. Cam and Elvira drove to Dallas in a Whippet motorcar that Leonard "L.L." Legters had given them. Cam's nephew Ron White went with them. He was interested in helping his Uncle Cam set up a campaign to teach as many Cakchiquel Indians as possible to read.

In Dallas, the Townsends met up with Lynn Van Sickle, since Cam had decided to present his idea for using airplanes to the mission leadership. The meeting did not go well. The leaders of Central American Mission were aghast when they learned the price tag for the project. The country was in the middle of a depression, they argued. Besides, Cam was talking about the Amazon Basin in *South* America, but their mission was to *Central* America, and Central America only.

Eventually, Cam managed to persuade the mission leaders to let him pursue the possibility of using an airplane. However, Cam could do this only on one condition: He would have to raise all of the money needed to buy and maintain an airplane.

Undaunted, Cam forged ahead. He knew the host of a Christian radio show in Dallas and asked if he could present the need for missionary airplanes to the show's audience. Cam was excited to be talking to so many Christians at one time on the air, and he did his best to explain why airplanes were needed. He felt sure that the recent deaths of two missionaries, a baby, and three Indian guides at the hands of a hostile tribe would help the public understand the need to get in and out of a remote area quickly. At the close of the broadcast, Cam invited the listeners to contribute towards a missionary airplane.

Over the next few days, Cam waited anxiously for a response. Finally, an envelope arrived in the mail. Cam ripped it open, and a single dollar fluttered out. Cam was a little discouraged by the response but was not yet ready to give up the idea.

Finally, Cam and Elvira, accompanied by Ron White and Lynn Van Sickle, set out for Guatemala in the Whippet. After an interesting drive through Mexico, they arrived in Guatemala City two days before Christmas 1930. They spent Christmas in the city with Cam's brother Paul and his wife and then headed with Ron for San Antonio. Lynn Van Sickle stayed behind in the city for his orientation into CAM missionary life.

Everyone in San Antonio was glad to see the Townsends again. It was a relief for the Indian church leaders to be able to speak to Cam in Cakchiquel instead of trying to talk with other CAM missionaries in fractured Spanish. The Townsends' foster daughter, Elena Trejo, was glad to have them back, too. Cam was impressed with how smart she was. She had learned everything the local schoolteachers could teach her, and it seemed a pity that her education should stop after grade school. Cam thought about what to do and then wrote to his parents in California asking if they would take care of Elena and enroll her in an American high school. Cam's parents wrote back immediately telling Cam they would be delighted to have Elena stay with them and to send her on up.

Cam continued his work among the Cakchiquel Christians and, with the help of his nephew Ron, planned a literacy campaign to teach as many Indians as possible to read and write in their own language. All the while, Cam waited for news that the Cakchiquel New Testaments had arrived in Guatemala City. But no news came.

Finally, in early May 1931, Cam and Trinidad Bac drove the Whippet over the mountains to Guatemala City to find out what had happened to the New Testaments. A worker at the central post office assured Cam he had not seen any package addressed to him. Cam, though, was not satisfied and asked if he could search through the back rooms. The worker shrugged his shoulders and agreed. Sure enough, Cam found a package addressed to him stuffed at the back of a shelf. Inside were the first eighteen copies of the Cakchiquel New Testament. Cam stood in the middle of the post office and thanked God for the book and all of the wonderful things it would do for the Cakchiquel people. He was eager to show it to the Cakchiquel Christians, but there was something he had to do first.

On May 19, 1931, Cameron Townsend, Trinidad Bac, and Mr. Gregory of the Bible Society stood outside the office of the president of Guatemala. At 4:30 P.M. sharp, President Ubico's secretary opened the door and ushered them in. President Ubico shook hands and greeted everyone warmly. Trinidad Bac then handed the president his own engraved copy of the Cakchiquel New Testament. Cam, Mr. Gregory, and Trinidad all gave short speeches, and then the president responded.

President Ubico congratulated all three of the men for the part they had played in getting the New Testament translated and published in the Cakchiquel language. He then invited Cam to begin work learning and translating the New Testament into another Indian language. The president also agreed to pose for a picture holding the copy of the New Testament, even though he usually avoided having his picture taken. The next morning, a photo of President Ubico holding the Cakchiquel New Testament appeared on the front page of Guatemala's leading newspaper.

Once the formalities of the official ceremony were completed, Cam was eager to get home to show the New Testament to the Cakchiquel Indians.

A crowd quickly gathered when Cam arrived back, and the people broke into loud applause when they saw the New Testament. Several of the local preachers who could read Cakchiquel took turns reading portions of the New Testament to the crowd. The Cakchiquel Indians decided that May 20 would be kept as a special day to commemorate receiving God's Word in their language.

The next day, Cam set out on an eleven-day mule trek through Cakchiquel territory to put the finishing touches on the plans for the literacy campaign. When he got back to Panajachel, where he and Elvira were staying in Robby Robinson's old house, he noticed a stranger in town. Cam introduced himself and learned that the man was a visitor from Mexico. Dr. Moisés Sáenz was Mexico's most famous champion of Indian education. His brother Aarón held a high position in the Mexican government. Cam had heard of both men and asked Dr. Sáenz what he was doing in such a remote village in Guatemala. Dr. Sáenz replied that he was studying the problems of rural Indian education in Central America in the hopes of finding some keys to help Mexican Indians get a better education.

Cam smiled to himself. Dr. Sáenz had come to just the right place! For the rest of the day, Cam showed the doctor around the Robinson Institute. Dr. Sáenz was very impressed to see fifty-three students studying hard. He questioned Cam on how he had managed to motivate these Indians to study. This was just the opening Cam had been waiting for. Cam told Dr. Sáenz how the Indians needed to be taught in their own language first and then in Spanish later, when they were older. By doing things in this order, the Indians could become proud of their heritage. Cam also explained how reading the Bible in their own language could set the Indians free from all the superstitions that had been keeping them ignorant and poor. They could then learn how to enter the mainstream of Guatemalan life on their own terms.

Dr. Sáenz snapped many photos of what he saw and wrote copious notes about what Cam was saying. When it was time to leave, he congratulated Cam on his work and invited him to come to Mexico and work among the Indians there.

When he returned to Mexico, Dr. Sáenz sent a formal letter to Cam inviting him to come and work in Mexico. It was the first of three letters Cam received that week, and it was the only one that contained good news. The second letter was from his sister to inform Cam that his mother had been diagnosed with cancer and was not expected to live long. The third letter arrived from the leaders of Central American Mission. It stated that since Cam and Elvira were the two missionaries who spoke Cakchiquel the best, it was the mission's recommendation that they stay in Guatemala and continue to work among the Cakchiquel Indians. A lot of time and money had been spent getting the Cakchiquels the New Testament in their own language, and now it was up to the Townsends to see that it was used to full advantage. The letter concluded with permission for Cam to do "occasional exploration into unoccupied fields."

At first Cam was very upset about the letter. He and Archer Anderson had spent years training Cakchiquel pastors at the Robinson Institute. Cam couldn't understand why the leaders of CAM thought the local pastors were less able to preach to their own people than he and the other American missionaries.

Cam did not have to decide how to respond to the letter. The decision was taken out of his hands when he went to see Dr. Ainslie complaining of chest pain and a cough that would not go away. The diagnosis was not good: tuberculosis, a lung disease that was often fatal. Dr. Ainslie told Cam his only chance to survive was to head back to the moderate climate of California, where he needed to get lots of rest. Even then, there were no guarantees that Cam would survive.

The Townsends quickly returned to California. They arrived soon after Cam's mother had died, and Cam and Elvira went to stay with Cam's sister Lula Griset and her family. The only joy for Cam being home under these circumstances was that he got to see Elena again. His foster daughter was doing well in high school and was living with Cam's father and sisters.

While the Townsends were staying with Lula, Elvira went for a routine medical checkup. Like Cam, she was feeling worn down and tired all the time. Since everyone assumed she had been working too hard looking after Cam, the diagnosis came as a shock. Elvira had a serious and untreatable heart condition that could kill her at any time. The doctor ordered total bed rest for her; she was not to get out of bed for anything except to go to the bathroom.

When Cam heard the diagnosis, he sat on the front porch of Lula's house in Santa Ana and wondered what had gone wrong. He had a great vision for reaching all the Indian tribes of Central and South America and giving them a Bible in their own language. But instead of being able to pursue his vision, he was holed up in a tiny house in California with tuberculosis and a wife who had a life-threatening heart condition. At that moment, it was hard for him to hold out much hope for the future.

Chapter 11

Links in a Chain

Lula took good care of her bedridden brother and sister-in-law. She prepared them meals made with farm-fresh vegetables and gave them both large glasses of fresh milk to drink. Slowly Cam's and Elvira's health began to improve.

As Cam got better, hope began to seep back into him. Cam started planning and strategizing in his mind again. By letter he communicated with many people, including Leonard "L.L." Legters, who had recently married a college professor. L.L. kept sending letters to Cam filled with all sorts of facts and information about the Indian tribes who did not have a written language. According to L.L., there were well over one thousand such tribes in the world, with fifty of them located in Mexico alone.

Cam's mind began to spin. There was no way he could meet the language needs of so many tribes on his own. After all, it had taken him ten years to translate the New Testament into the Cakchiquel language. Using airplanes was a part of the solution, Cam was sure of that, but the bigger part of the solution was people. Thousands of missionaries needed to be trained to do translation work. Cam knew of two universities in the United States that offered courses in linguistics, but they were four-year courses and didn't address the area of writing down a previously unwritten language. As he thought about it, Cam told himself there was only one solution. Somehow he would have to start a linguistics school to train missionaries and then send them out to work in areas where they would be the most useful.

Cam wrote to L.L. about this, and L.L. wrote back a very encouraging letter. Why not start in Mexico, he suggested. Mexico was close to the United States, and the fifty unwritten languages there would give the missionaries plenty of opportunity to practice their newly acquired linguistics skills.

Cam liked the idea. He had seen how linguists could get into places where normal missionaries were not welcome. He began to imagine what it would be like if every tribe on earth had access to the Bible and other books in their own language.

By the summer of 1933, Cam was feeling much better and was ready to put his plan into action. He was going to train linguists at a camp right in Mexico and then send them out to nearby tribes to learn the various local languages. He even had a name in mind for the group: Wycliffe Bible Translators, named for John Wycliffe, who had translated the Bible from Latin into English so that peasants and workers could read and understand it for themselves. As Cam read about John Wycliffe, he was surprised to discover that English was the thirty-third language the Bible had been translated into. He wondered where the English-speaking world would be without the diligent translation work of John Wycliffe.

While Cam had the vision and name for this new endeavor, there was one problem with the plan. The Mexican government was cracking down on all religious activity in the country. It had been fifteen years since Mexico's revolution, and one of the goals of the revolution had been to take power away from the Roman Catholic Church. As a result, all religious schools had been taken over by the government, as well as all property belonging to the Catholic Church. Protestant missionaries were also being watched carefully, and no new missionaries were being issued visas to enter Mexico. All in all, Mexico seemed a bleak place in which to start the new program.

When L.L. visited Cam in Santa Ana with his wife, he encouraged Cam not to worry about the situation in Mexico. Somehow, L.L. assured Cam, God would work it all out.

After visiting Cam, the Legterses traveled on to a large Keswick Bible Conference in New Jersey, where L.L. and James Dale, a missionary from

Mexico, were the main speakers. On the second day of the conference, James Dale spoke about the problems facing missionaries in Mexico. After he finished speaking, those attending the conference spent the rest of the day praying and fasting for Mexico. Indeed, many people stayed up all night and prayed. The following morning, everyone at the conference urged L.L. to go with Cam to Mexico and help him set up a training camp for Bible translators. They were all sure that God would clear the way for them to enter the country despite being missionaries. One woman even donated a car to L.L. so that he could get to Mexico, and another person gave him gas money.

L.L. decided to take up the challenge. As soon as the conference was over, he wrote to Cam telling him of his decision. The two of them agreed to meet in Dallas, Texas, and travel on to Mexico from there.

Elvira was still not well, and Cam arranged for her to travel to Chicago to stay with her family while he was in Mexico.

Cam arrived in Dallas a couple of days ahead of schedule. He wanted to meet with the leaders of Central American Mission. After the meeting, Karl Hummel, secretary of the mission, was traveling to Wichita Falls for a two-day visit, and he invited Cam to accompany him. Since Cam had nothing else to do but wait for L.L. to arrive, he accepted the invitation. While Cam was in Wichita Falls, the rector at a local Episcopal church heard about him and asked him to visit. Cam wondered why he had been invited to the rector's home. The rector had visited Mexico several years before and had become fascinated by the religion of the ancient Aztecs. It appeared to Cam he had been invited to listen to the rector lecture him on the subject, and he sat and listened politely, offering an occasional comment when he could. Finally, the rector seemed to run out of things to say, and the two men sat in silence for a few moments. Suddenly the rector jumped to his feet. "I nearly forgot," he exclaimed. "I'm going to give you the address of the Episcopal dean of Mexico City. Here," he said, pulling a business card from a desk drawer. "Let me write you a quick introduction. The dean has some influential friends if you ever need help."

The rector took a pen and scratched a few words of introduction on the back of the card before handing it to Cam.

"Thank you," said Cam as he took the card and then shook the rector's hand. "It has been a pleasure to meet you. I hope to see you in Mexico one day."

The rector smiled. "Thank you for coming. I enjoyed our little chat."

As Cam walked down the path away from the rector's home, he had no idea of the value of the scribbled message on the back of the card in his coat pocket. It alone was worth the two-day visit to Wichita Falls.

When Cam returned to Dallas, L.L. and his wife Edna were waiting for him. The next day it was time to start the drive south to the Mexican border and see whether they would be allowed into the country. The three of them reached the border at Laredo on November 11, 1933. They entered the building housing Mexican Immigration and explained to the official there why they wanted to enter his country.

"No, no!" shouted the official in rapid Spanish. "We have too much of your religion already. I will not stamp your passports. You must go back."

Cam looked from L.L. to Edna. Both had surprised looks on their faces. "May we sit down?" Cam asked the official.

"Help yourself," sneered the official, pointing towards some hardwood chairs clumped in the corner, "but you're wasting your time."

As the hours rolled by, it did indeed seem as if the three of them were wasting their time. L.L. sat humming the same Christian chorus over and over while his wife stared out the window at the muddy Rio Grande that separated Texas from Mexico. Cam alternated between nervously fiddling with his briefcase and praying silently. Every half hour or so he would try talking to the official again, and each time the official seemed to be ruder than the time before. He wanted to know why they hadn't left the building yet. They sat waiting, but for what? he demanded to know.

Suddenly Cam had a flash of inspiration. He pulled his briefcase out from under the chair and began rummaging through it. He grabbed a stack of papers and flicked through them. "Yes!" he exclaimed. "Read this, L.L. I think it might be the answer."

L.L. took the sheet of paper and began to read. "Who is Moisés Sáenz?" he asked.

"They call him the father of Mexican education," said Cam excitedly. "And his brother is the mayor of Mexico City. Remember, I told you how he visited Panajachel and how he was excited about the work we were doing and invited me to come and work in Mexico with him."

"Amazing!" replied L.L. "And you've been carrying this invitation in your briefcase the whole time?"

Cam nodded. "I have so many papers stuffed in there I didn't even think of it until just now. Come on, let's show it to the official."

Cam and L.L. hurried to the counter. The official gave them the same bored look he had given them before. Cam handed him the letter. "Sir," he said, "I believe you might like to see the invitation I have to visit your country."

The official scowled, but when he saw the government seal on the paper his mouth dropped open. He hurried into a back room, beckoning several colleagues to follow him. They stayed in the room for nearly an hour, and every so often Cam could hear raised voices. Eventually, the official emerged and cleared his throat. "Mr. Townsend and Mr. and Mrs. Legters," he said, bowing slightly, "I have been in contact with my superiors, and in light of this letter we are pleased to welcome you to our country.

There are just two things we must ask you to refrain from doing. You must not preach your religion or study any Indian languages. If you do you will be fined and deported. Other than that, you are free to do as you please. Give me your passports please, and I will stamp them."

The three of them handed over their passports, and within half an hour they were bumping their way along the half-constructed Pan American highway towards Monterrey, where they planned to spend the night.

A gloom settled over Cam and the Legterses during the next few days. Sure, they were in Mexico, but they were forbidden to do what they had come for. However, over the course of the next week, they learned how big a concession the Mexican immigration officials had made on their behalf. Everywhere they turned, missionaries related stories of being thrown out of towns and told to return home. James Dale's son Johnny, who had been born in Mexico, could not get a resident's visa, even after spending hundreds of dollars on attorney's fees. As the days rolled by, the three of them began to lose hope. In Mexico City they discovered that Dr. Sáenz, who would have surely helped them, was in the United States lecturing, and he would not be back for another two months. By the end of their third week in Mexico, the Legterses were ready to go home.

"You can stay here if you like," L.L. said to Cam, "but I have other things I could be doing at home.

All the paperwork we have to do could take months, and even then there's no guarantee they'll let us do missionary work here."

Cam understood how his friend felt, but something inside him told him to hold on. "God has brought us this far, and He will carry us on," he encouraged L.L.

A few days later, they got the break they were looking for. Once again Cam remembered something in his briefcase. This time it was the business card from the Episcopal rector in Wichita Falls, Texas. In the hopes of meeting the Episcopal dean of Mexico City, Cam decided to attend the morning service at the cathedral the following Sunday.

As it happened, the dean was preaching that Sunday morning, and he stood at the door shaking hands with the congregation after the service. Cam introduced himself and gave the dean the card with the introduction scribbled on the back. After reading it, the dean looked impressed. He invited Cam to come to dinner the following Tuesday night.

Cam rushed back to tell the Legterses what had happened. They prayed together that somehow the dinner on Tuesday night would help them find a way to do what they had come to Mexico to do.

Tuesday night quickly rolled around, and at dinner with the dean that night Cam found himself seated next to Dr. Bernard Bevans, a British ethnologist (a person who studied different peoples and races) whom Cam found to be very interesting. The two men were soon swapping stories about working with rural Indians. By the end of the evening, Dr. Bevans had made plans for a lunch meeting with some of his friends who he was sure would be interested in the work Cam had been doing in Guatemala and was now planning to do in Mexico.

Again, it was a matter of waiting, but Cam felt he was getting closer to a breakthrough. On Friday he walked to the exclusive Lady Baltimore Dining Room, where Dr. Bevans had arranged for the lunch meeting to be held. One of the first people Cam met there was Dr. Frank Tannenbaum from Columbia University in New York City. As they talked, several people came up to congratulate Dr. Tannenbaum on his new book titled *Peace by Revolution*. Looking for any opportunity that might help, Cam sneaked out of the luncheon and ran to the nearest bookstore. He hurriedly purchased a copy of Dr. Tannenbaum's book and ran back to the dining room before anyone missed him.

Cam spotted Dr. Tannenbaum right where he had left him talking to an elderly man. When he was finished talking, Cam went up to him. "Dr. Tannenbaum," he said, "I would be very honored if you would autograph my copy of *Peace by Revolution*. I admire it very much."

Dr. Tannenbaum looked flattered. "Of course I will, Mr. Townsend, and may I say I admire your work among the Indians in Guatemala. You have very innovative ideas—most interesting indeed," he said, writing away in the front of the book. "There, I hope we meet up again. I know it's difficult to get anything done in Mexico right now. Everyone is very suspicious of foreigners. Let me write a note of introduction for you to a friend of mine, Rafael Ramírez. He is a progressive thinker and the head of rural education for the country. I believe he's on a tour of schools right now, but he will be in Monterrey on the twenty-third."

Cam watched as Dr. Tannenbaum wrote a note of introduction to Rafael Ramírez and then handed it to him. He thanked the doctor very much for the gesture.

It was not until he arrived back at the room he was renting that Cam read what Dr. Tannenbaum had written in the front of the book along with his autograph. It was several sentences commending Cam on his good work among the rural Indians and urging him to keep it up. Cam smiled to himself as he started reading the book, with the hope that he was another step closer to getting permission to do missionary work in Mexico.

On the twenty-third, Cam and L.L. were in Monterrey waiting for Rafael Ramírez to arrive. When señor Ramírez finally stepped out of a car and onto the pavement in front of the government building, Cam introduced himself and told him why he had come to Mexico. He then handed Dr. Tannenbuam's note of introduction to him.

The director of rural education looked frustrated and ran his hand over his graying hair as he read the note. "I don't know what I'm supposed to do for you," he said. "The Indians have far too much religion already."

Cam thought quickly. "You're right," he agreed. "The Indians do have too much superstition and religion, but what they've never had is the opportunity to read the Bible for themselves in their own language. That, sir, is the key to encouraging them to be good citizens."

Rafael Ramírez looked startled. "I've never thought of it that way," he admitted. "But we can't bring in people to do translation work, and even if the Bible were translated, there's no way we could allow you to distribute it." As he spoke, his eyes settled on the book under Cam's arm. "Ah," he said, sounding relieved to change the subject. "I see you have a copy of Dr. Tannenbaum's book. What an insightful man he is. One of the few Americans who truly understand the aims of the Mexican revolution."

Cam smiled. "I couldn't agree more," he said. "In fact, I met Dr. Tannenbaum only last week." He opened the book to the front page. "I explained my work to him, and he wrote me a note. Wasn't that thoughtful of him?"

"Yes," agreed Rafael Ramírez, craning his neck to read the endorsement. As he did so, he began to smile broadly. "Mr. Townsend, perhaps I have been too quick in my judgment of you," he apologized. "If Dr. Tannenbaum thinks you know what you are doing with rural Indian education, who am I to stand in your way? I cannot allow you to do Bible translation work, of course, but you do have my permission to study rural education in Mexico. Perhaps you might even be able to offer some suggestions for improvement. How would that be?" he flashed a smile at Cam. "If you come to my office tomorrow morning, I will have all the paperwork ready for you."

"Thank you," said Cam gratefully. "That would be wonderful."

Ten minutes later, Cam and L.L. sat discussing the invitation to study rural education. It was not everything they had hoped for, but it was a start. As they talked, Cam thought back over the events that had brought him this far: the business card from the Episcopal rector, the invitation to dinner by the Episcopal dean of Mexico City, the invitation to lunch by Dr. Bevans, Dr. Tannenbaum's endorsement in the front of his book, and now permission from Rafael Ramírez, director of rural education in Mexico, to go out among the Indian tribes and observe the work of rural schools. They were all links in a chain, and Cam had the faith to believe that somehow the chain would continue and eventually he would be allowed to bring Bible translators into Mexico.

Chapter 12

Camp Wycliffe

For the next six weeks, Cam toured rural Indian schools in the states of Chiapas, Campeche, Tabasco, Veracruz, Morelos, Oaxaca, and Yucatan. He took notes on everything he saw, from the types of textbooks used to the amount of training teachers had received. Overall he was impressed by what he saw. The schools in Mexico still had a long way to go, but the government was making a real effort to improve the lot of Indians in the country. Everywhere Cam went, the letter of introduction from Rafael Ramírez made him an instant honored guest. As he traveled, Cam found himself impressed with some of the results of the Mexican Revolution. In 1922, there had been only 309 public schools in the country; now, eleven years later, there were 7,504 public schools.

Sadly, Cam's tour of rural schools was cut short when he received a telegram from Chicago informing him that Elvira was seriously ill and not expected to live more than a few days. Cam wanted to get to his wife's side as fast as he could, but he didn't have the money for a plane ticket, so he climbed aboard a train headed for the U.S. border. The train was slow, and as Cam sat surrounded by Mexican people in the second-class carriage, he prayed that Elvira would hold on until he got to her.

Once in the United States, Cam caught another train to Sulphur Springs, Arkansas, where his brother Paul was now director at the John Brown Academy. Paul loaned Cam a car, and as quickly as he could, Cam drove to Chicago. He found Elvira alive but very weak. She could barely lift her head off the pillow. When she saw Cam, she begged him to take her to the mountains. Cam arranged blankets and pillows in the back seat of the car and gently helped his wife into the car. He then drove to the Ozark Mountains to stay with Dr. Bast and his wife, who were good friends of Paul Townsend's.

Under Dr. Bast's constant care, Elvira began to make a slow recovery. As she recovered, Cam made the most of the opportunity to rest, taking long, leisurely strolls through the woods. It was spring in the Ozarks, the wild apple trees were in blossom, and the air was alive with the cries of mocking-birds as they busily built their nests.

Cam's body might have rested, but his mind did not. It was as active as ever. Cam thought about all he had seen in Mexico, and he wrote some articles on the state of rural education there. The articles were published in the *Dallas News* newspaper and *School and Society* magazine. Much to his surprise, Cam received a letter from Rafael Ramírez congrat-ulating him on his understanding of rural education in Mexico. Somehow Cam's articles had found their way to Rafael's office.

Cam also started thinking again about the training school in linguistics. As he walked through the woods, he became convinced it was time to begin such a school. Then the thought struck him: Why not hold the school right there in the Ozark Mountains? For the next month, Cam thought about little else than the form a linguistics school should take. He wrote many letters to Christians who had shown an interest in linguis-tics, from college professors to elderly women in his home church who had promised to pray for him daily.

Then one Monday morning early in April 1934, Cam sat down at his typewriter and rolled several sheets of blank paper separated by layers of carbon paper into the machine. He was ready to type up the prospectus for his linguistics school. It read:

SUMMER TRAINING CAMP
FOR PROSPECTIVE BIBLE TRANSLATORS

June 7–Sept. 7, 1934

Happy Valley Farm,
Sulphur Springs, Arkansas

TEACHERS AND SUBJECTS
TO BE COVERED AS TIME PERMITS:

L. L. Legters: Indian Distribution and Tribal
                         History
                      Indian Customs and Psychology
                      Indian Evangelization and
                         Spiritual Development
                      How to Get Guidance
                      How to Work with Others

J. M. Chicol: Spanish
                      Indian Orthography and
                         Pronunciation
                      Indian Superstitions, Vices and
                         Religions

W. C. Townsend: Economic and Cultural Status
                         of the Indians
                      Governmental Programs
                         Regarding Indians
                      Indian Translation—Field
                         Problems

Indian Philology
Why and How of Reading
Campaigns

Paul Townsend: Indian Workers' Practical
Living Problems

Some notions will also be given regarding the geography and history of Latin America and it is hoped that we can secure Frank C. Pinkerton, M.D., for courses on Keeping Well in the Tropics, First Aid, and Indian Archaeology, and Dr. E. L. McCreery for a short course on Phonetics. Where the word Indian *is used it refers to the Indians of Latin America.*

Cam typed up something else, too—a letter to Will Nyman, head of the missionary committee at the Church of the Open Door in Los Angeles. It was not an easy letter for Cam to write. The church had supported him financially for seventeen years. In the letter, Cam asked them to find another missionary to give their money to, though he still asked for the church's prayer support. He had thought about this decision long and hard and finally decided it would be best for him to enter a country as a linguist, someone who wanted to translate native languages. If he was asked where his money came from, he wanted to be able to say that concerned friends and family members helped out with gifts rather than that he was on the "payroll" of a church, no matter how lean that payroll might be!

Over the next month, Cam made several visits to Christian colleges in the area looking for students who wanted to be part of his first summer linguistics program. He handed out copies of the prospectus after class, often staying late into the evening to answer people's questions. And there were plenty of questions, since no one had ever run a program quite like this before. Most prospective students wanted to know where they would be living if they came and what they would be doing. Cam pulled no punches. He told them one of the objectives of the camp was to weed out anyone who could not stand up to the harsh living conditions they would encounter in some of the remote and primitive areas where the Bible needed to be translated.

On Thursday, June 7, 1934, Cam Townsend surveyed the scene before him. Sitting on nail kegs in the front yard of a sparsely furnished farmhouse were seven people. The teachers outnumbered the students two to one! Richmond McKinney from Dallas Theological Seminary and Ed Sywulka from Columbia Bible College in South Carolina were the only two students who had responded to the prospectus and enrolled in the school. Joe Chicol, Paul Townsend, Leonard Legters, and, of course, Cam were there as teachers. Elvira, whose health had improved some, was there to support the group in any way she could.

Cam was excited. He didn't care how few people showed up. The point was that Camp Wycliffe had begun. And the camp turned out to be every bit as tough as Cam had promised it would be. There were no beds, only the wooden floor to sleep on, softened with cut grass, if the students decided to cut it. There was no indoor plumbing. Water had to be pumped from a well, and everyone took turns preparing meals from the produce grown on the farm. There was not much money to buy anything else. Occasionally someone in Cam's family would send Cam a few dollars, which he shared with the group. Or sometimes one of the staff would be invited to speak at a nearby church, for which he received a small offering. This money, too, was shared with the group. No one seemed to mind that money was in short supply or that food choices were fairly limited. There was so much to learn in such a short time that no one had time to worry about his stomach.

Near the end of the three-month school, Cam received a letter informing him that Dr. McCreery, a former missionary to Africa and teacher at the Bible Institute of Los Angeles (Biola), would not be able to make it to the camp after all. Dr. McCreery had commitments in California that he could not break. At first Cam was disappointed because both Richmond McKinney and Ed Sywulka needed more training in phonetics. Then he struck on an idea. If Dr. McCreery couldn't come to them, why not send the young men to Dr. McCreery? Cam quickly wrote to his old friend Will Nyman, who lived in Glendale, California, and asked if he would be willing to host the two students while they studied with Dr. McCreery in Los Angeles.

Will wrote right back. The young men were welcome to stay with his family for as long as they needed. On their trip to Los Angeles, Cam arranged for Richmond and Ed to stay with various missionaries living on Indian reservations. He wanted them to be aware that there were many native groups inside the boundaries of the United States who spoke little or no English and were in need of a written language of their own.

The plan worked without a hitch, and in September 1934, the two students graduated and Camp Wycliffe was declared a success.

Once the school was over, Cam and Elvira set off for Mexico. Getting across the border wasn't any trouble this time. The trouble started inside Mexico. The couple drove down the Pan American highway as far as Monterrey. From there they planned to head south to Mexico City but were hampered from doing so by huge landslides that blocked the road. Since there was no way around the landslides, Cam and Elvira waited in Monterrey for eight weeks while the road was repaired. The strain of it all aggravated Elvira's condition, and once again a doctor told Cam his wife was about to die. He advised Cam to begin making plans for Elvira's funeral, since many permits would be needed to hold a religious service in the city.

In the end, Cam decided it would be best to take Elvira home to the people who knew and loved her.

He gassed up the car and headed north to Dallas. Back home, many people helped take care of Elvira, and Cam found himself with some time to think about the future. His heart was still set on helping Indians. As he thought about the way to help them, he came upon an interesting idea. Why not write a novel that would show the hardships of life for the Indians of Central America? Perhaps people who would not come to a church to hear Cam speak about the needs of Indians in Central America would be interested enough to read a novel about the Indians' hardships. Cam pulled out his typewriter and began immediately.

Four months later, *Tolo, the Volcano's Son* was finished. Cam called it fiction, but the book was really based on many of the people he had lived and worked with in San Antonio. He showed the manuscript to the editor of a magazine called *Revelation,* (today called *Eternity),* and the editor agreed to publish the story in the magazine as a serial, one chapter a month.

By now it was winter, and Cam began promoting the second linguistics school, to be held in the summer of 1935. He typed another prospectus and wrote hundreds of letters contacting anyone he thought might be remotely interested in attending. His persistence paid off. There had been two students in 1934, but five students signed up for the 1935 school. This time, the number of students would equal the number of teachers.

Chapter 13

South to Mexico

Once again, Cam welcomed each student to Camp Wycliffe. The first two to arrive were Brainerd Legters and Max Lathrop. Brainerd was L.L.'s son. He had just finished seminary in Philadelphia and had convinced fellow student Maxwell Lathrop to attend the camp with him. The two planned to go on to Mexico after the school if they could get visas.

Next to arrive was Richmond McKinney, who had returned for his second year at Camp Wycliffe. Then came Bill Sedat, a young, blond German-born student. The last to arrive was Ken Pike, who had hitchhiked all the way from Boston because he did not have enough money for the train fare. Ken Pike came with his heart set on becoming a missionary.

Indeed, he had already applied twice to the China Inland Mission, and both times had been turned down. According to the China Inland Mission his health was "too fragile" for them to accept him. Cam had to admit that Ken was very thin and pale. Ken looked like he'd never spent a day in the sun in his life.

Still, Cam had suffered from tuberculosis and had a wife with a serious heart condition. As a result, he had promised himself he would never turn down a person on the basis of his or her health. He reasoned that if God wanted the person to become a missionary, who was he to stand in the way?

Camp Wycliffe was run much the same as it had been the year before. The students sat on the same nail kegs and took notes from the same lecturers. There were also chores to do every day, and each student learned outdoor survival techniques. On the second day of camp, the men were asked to gather dry firewood so that they could cook dinner over an open fire. Cam and L.L. watched in amazement as Ken Pike hurried off and climbed a nearby tree.

"What on earth does he think he's doing?" asked Cam. "You don't find firewood up a tree. You find it on the ground."

L.L. shook his head and muttered, "Lord, couldn't you have sent us someone better than this?"

Cam chuckled. "You should hear him imitating Cakchiquel sounds, though. I tell you, Ken might not win any outdoor awards, but he has potential as a linguist."

This time around, Dr. McCreery was able to come to Arkansas to lecture at Camp Wycliffe. Everyone, including Cam and Elvira, took copious notes as he spoke. During one of his sessions, Dr. McCreery suggested they hold a special day of prayer and ask God to open the doors into Mexico so that the students would be able to work freely in the country.

This was no small matter. Since the election of Lázaro Cárdenas as president of Mexico, the noose had been tightening around the necks of missionaries. President Cárdenas had chosen many atheists to be in his cabinet, and they had put in place harsh new laws aimed at stopping missionary work altogether. One law banned religious material from being sent by mail. Thousands of Spanish Bibles had been seized as a result of the law, and missionaries were not even allowed to send out their monthly newsletters. Another law made it nearly impossible for a missionary to obtain a visa to enter the country, let alone stay there.

July 24, 1935, was set aside to pray for Mexico. In the morning, the students and staff gathered around on their usual nail keg seats and listened as Cam outlined the already familiar state of affairs in Mexico. As the morning progressed, everyone got down on his knees and asked God to open the doors into Mexico so that they could all go there and work among the Indian tribes and do their translation work unhindered.

Cam was still outside praying at lunchtime when one of the students tuned in the large valve radio in the dining room to hear the midday news. "Come and hear this!" he yelled to the others.

Everyone raced into the dining room and gathered around the radio. The news announcer spoke in a booming voice. "And now for an update on the political situation in Mexico," he said. "Only minutes ago, President Lázaro Cárdenas announced a major shake-up in his government. He has dismissed his entire cabinet, saying he wishes to build a new one with more moderate views."

A cheer went up from the group. "It's amazing!" declared Cam.

Indeed, the change was amazing. Each night over the next two weeks, the news described the developments unfolding in Mexico. President Cárdenas appointed a new cabinet and struck down many of the harsh antireligious laws. The ban on mailing religious material was lifted. New immigration laws allowing missionaries to stay in the country for longer periods of time were announced. Most exciting of all, the president recommended that translators be invited to the country to work among the Indian tribes!

The Mexican government had made a 180° turn in favor of missionaries. Cam could hardly wait for the classroom stage of Camp Wycliffe to be over so that they could all head south and try their hand at translation.

By mid-August, everyone in the school was ready for the trip south to Mexico, where the students planned to begin working with six unwritten languages. Some of the students planned to stay in Mexico until the task was done, while others planned to return to the United States in the fall to continue with their regular courses of study.

Cam had been very concerned about taking Elvira south again, but his niece Evelyn Griset offered to travel with them and act as a nurse and companion for her aunt. That took care of the worries about Elvira, but Cam fretted about where they would live once they got to Mexico. Given Elvira's condition, he felt she needed something more substantial than a cornstalk house to live in. This problem, too, was taken care of. Tom Haywood, a local Christian businessman, had a washing machine sitting around the house. In 1935, a washing machine was a fairly valuable item. Tom traded the machine for an old house trailer, which he gave to Cam and Elvira for them to tow to Mexico to use as a house.

Cam was delighted with the house trailer. It had a tank for running water and a pull-out table and chairs. It had just one drawback: It weighed nearly two tons. The trailer might make it to Mexico, but Cam's car towing it might not. The car was an old relic that hardly went twenty miles without breaking down. Still, there was little Cam could do about it. Since he had no money to buy a new car, he took the old car to the blacksmith's workshop and asked the blacksmith to attach a trailer hitch.

A local pastor had heard about the situation and gave Cam his car. Although the car would not tow the monstrous trailer either, the pastor was sure that Cam could trade it and his old car for one large enough to pull the house trailer to Mexico. He was right. Cam traded the two cars in for an old Buick. The car used almost as much oil as it did gas—about a quart every twenty-five miles—but it was solid enough to tow the trailer, and that was what mattered.

Cam had everything he needed now, and he and Elvira and Evelyn Griset climbed eagerly into the old Buick. They were finally headed for Mexico, and nothing was going to stand in their way. The rest of those in the school had gone on ahead in a second car.

There were many stops along the way to top up the oil, but eventually the trio made it to Dallas, where they spent several nights as guests of Central American Mission. Then it was on to Laredo and the Mexican border. The travelers did not have any-where near the sixty dollars per person per month that Mexican Immigration required foreign visitors entering the country to have. Cam, though, did not worry. He believed that something would work out.

And so it did. As Cam drove up to the border, all the Mexican immigration officials there came out to meet him, their mouths agape in wonder. They had never seen anything like it before. "A house with wheels!" they exclaimed, walking around the car and house trailer when Cam pulled to a halt.

As always, Cam saw an opportunity. "Yes," he said, climbing out of the driver's seat. "My family is going to live in it while we work with the Indian people. Would you like to see inside?"

One by one the immigration officials clambered into the trailer, chattering away in rapid Spanish as they examined everything.

When all the paperwork had been done and the passports had been stamped with visas, Cam wished the officials well and climbed back into the car. As he drove off, the immigration officials stood and waved good-bye, so in awe of the huge house trailer that they seemed to have forgotten to ask Cam how much money he had on him.

"What about the money, Uncle Cam? Did they want to see it?" asked Evelyn as they bumped along the road.

Cam looked back and smiled. "Didn't even ask. Praise God, I think this is going to be a trip to remember!"

The car and house trailer made slow progress along the Pan American Highway. It seemed to Cam that every five miles or so there was road construction they had to stop for. Finally, near the village of Tamazunchale, there was no way through the construction. Workers were blasting a cutting for the road through solid rock. There was nothing for the trio to do but wait until the way was clear. A local missionary took them in and provided a place to stay. It was a week before word came that the road would be opened for a few hours to let traffic through.

Cam was glad to be on his way again, but not for long! As he rounded a bend, there in front of him was a steep, muddy road. Something inside him told him there was no way the car would make it up the slippery hill, but Cam had little choice but to try. There was no other way to get to Mexico City by car. Sure enough, about halfway up the slope, the wheels of the Buick began to spin in the mud. In his rearview mirror, Cam could see clods of mud spewing out from the back wheels. He gripped the steering wheel tightly as he began to lose control of the Buick and the trailer it was pulling. Slowly, unavoidably, they were sliding towards the side of the road—and the edge of the cliff that lay just beyond it. As they slid, the car jackknifed slightly, sending the rear right wheel over the edge first. They all held their breath, waiting for the fall—but it didn't come. Instead, the Buick teetered on the edge, its back wheels dangling over a three-hundred-foot precipice.

It took Cam a few seconds to realize that the car wasn't going over the cliff right away. "Get out the left side of the car as smoothly as you can," he told Elvira and Evelyn. His voice was calm, but his stomach was tied in knots. Slowly, he opened the driver's-side door and stepped out onto the muddy road. He hugged Elvira, who by then was white with fright. The three of them backed away from the Buick and the edge of the cliff. A construction worker was operating a grader a little farther up the road, and Cam managed to persuade him to tow the Buick back onto the road and away from the edge of disaster.

The three of them continued on their way, and although the Buick did slide several more times on the muddy stretch of road, it never slid close to the edge of the cliff again.

Several days later, when the twin volcanoes of Popo and Ixta came into view, Cam knew they were near Mexico City. He was not looking forward to navigating the Buick towing the huge trailer through the narrow streets of the capital to Coyoacan, their destination on the other side of the city.

"I had better pull off here before we get into heavy traffic," Cam told Elvira as they arrived in Villa de Guadalupe, a suburb on the outskirts of Mexico City. "I'd like to check the trailer coupling and put some more oil in the car. The last thing we need is to have the car break down in traffic."

Evelyn agreed, handing her uncle a bottle of oil as he climbed out of the Buick. "There are only three bottles of oil left, Uncle Cam," she added.

Cam lifted the Buick's hood and was just about to unscrew the oil cap when he looked up and saw two Mexican motorcycle police officers coming to a stop beside the car.

"Having a problem, señor?" the taller of the two officers asked Cam.

"No," replied Cam. "I was just putting some oil in the engine and checking the trailer coupling. I'm getting ready to drive across the city. How is the traffic?"

The police officers looked at each other. "You are an American?" the tall one asked.

"Yes," replied Cam. "I'm from California, and I'm here in your country to teach rural Indians to read the Word of God in their own languages."

The shorter officer smiled a broad smile and switched to speaking in English. "I was privileged to visit your state last year as a member of the Mexican shooting team. The chief of police in the town where we were staying was very hospitable to us, as were many other Americans we met along the way. It would be my pleasure to return some of that hospitality to you. Follow us. We will escort you across the city."

"Thank you very much," responded Cam, not sure what they meant by the offer. He poured the oil into the engine and closed the hood. The two police officers smiled as Cam climbed back into the Buick. Cam started the car and gave a wave to signal he was ready. The officers kick-started their motorcycles.

Cam was telling Elvira and Evelyn what the police officers had said when the motorbike sirens began to wail. The officers looked back grinning and waved Cam on. Cam guided the Buick hauling the house trailer away from the curb and followed the two motorcycles. On both sides of the road, buses screeched to a halt, cars and horse-drawn wagons stopped dead, and trucks piled high with produce pulled to the side of the road. Cam laughed out loud. He was in Mexico City, and he felt like Moses parting the Red Sea as he made his way effortlessly through the traffic.

Chapter 14

Tetelcingo

Cam could not have planned things better if he had tried. His arrival in Mexico City coincided with the start of the two-week-long Seventh Inter-American Scientific Congress. This was an annual event where officials from all over Central America gathered to explore ways to improve the lot of the people in their countries. At the 1935 congress, the main topic on the agenda was to be how to promote the use of Indian languages. As soon as Cam had dispatched the Camp Wycliffe students to their various assignments around the country, he went straight downtown to the Palace of Fine Arts, where the congress had been convened. When he arrived there, he was recognized by a number of the congress delegates from Guatemala who

147

invited him to take part in the various forums being held.

During the congress, Cam met many important people who showed great interest in and support for his work. Among them were Mexico's secretary of labor, the founder and director of the Mexican Institute of Linguistic Investigations, and his old friend Rafael Ramírez, the director of rural education in Mexico. Each man enthusiastically endorsed Cam's work and introduced Cam to many other government officials present at the congress.

On the final day, President Cárdenas addressed the congress. He did not sound to Cam at all like the radical reformer who had banned missionaries from Mexico when he first came to power. Indeed, the president seemed to be a sincere and concerned man who had the good of all Mexican people at heart. He was the first Mexican president to really concern himself with the welfare of the poorest Indians in the country, so much so that he had been nicknamed the "peasant's president." President Cárdenas, a small man with dark black hair and a neatly trimmed mustache, was himself part Indian. Cam wished he could meet and speak personally to the president, but he knew it was impossible. There were so many other important men at the congress for President Cárdenas to talk to. Little did Cam know then that one day the president would come to speak with him!

By the time the Seventh Inter-American Scientific Congress was over, Cam had been issued a challenge. There was an Aztec-speaking village sixty miles outside Mexico City in the state of Morelos. Although the village was only a mile from the highway, its one thousand inhabitants were said to be the poorest in all of Morelos. A government official suggested Cam begin his translation work there so that everyone could see the kind of difference having the Bible in their own language would make to the people of the village.

Cam discussed the idea with Elvira and Evelyn. They got out a map of Mexico and found Morelos and then the village of Tetelcingo, located due south and situated three thousand feet lower than Mexico City. The elevation was much better for Elvira's heart condition, and they would be only a mile from the main highway should Elvira need urgent medical help. It all seemed to fit together perfectly. Cam poured another quart of oil into the Buick's engine and hitched up the house trailer.

Several hours later, Cam brought the old Buick with the heavy house trailer behind it to a halt. He was parked at the edge of the large dirt square in the center of Tetelcingo. Within moments, swarms of half-dressed, barefoot children emerged from the dust and surrounded the car. The children giggled and shouted to one another, but Cam could not understand a word they said. Gently he opened the car door and climbed out. Hoping someone would understand him, he announced in Spanish, "I would like to see the mayor."

Sure enough, a short, square-faced man wearing the traditional white muslin suit and serape (the Mexican shawl men wore over one shoulder) stepped forward. Cam noticed he had a gun tucked in his belt. "I am the mayor," said the man in perfect Spanish.

Cam smiled broadly. "Then you are just the man I have come to talk to," he exclaimed. "But before anything else, please tell me how you say good day in your language so I can greet you properly."

"Shimopanotli," said the man, looking puzzled.

"Shimopanotli," Cam replied, pulling a small notebook from his pocket and writing the word down. He then turned to the children. "Shimopanotli," he said to them. The children laughed and elbowed each other.

The mayor chuckled, too. "I must say, no stranger has ever wanted to know how to talk like us. My name is Martin Méndez. What can I do for you, señor?"

Cam watched out of the corner of his eye as two piglets chased each other under the house trailer. "My wife and niece are in the car. We would like to live in your village," he said.

Shock registered on the mayor's face. "For what purpose?" he questioned.

"I would like to learn your language and write it down for you," said Cam simply. "I have some official papers for you to look at."

Cam reached into the car and pulled out his briefcase. He clicked the case open and pulled out some letters of recommendation a number of officials had written for him. "You speak excellent Spanish," he commented as he handed the letters to the mayor.

Martin Méndez nodded. "Thank you," he replied. "I am the only good Spanish speaker in the village. I served in Zapata's army for eleven years, and I had to learn Spanish then. Now it comes in useful from time to time." He paused to read the letters of recommendation.

"Well," he said when he finished reading, "you are very welcome to live in our humble village. Do you intend to live in the house on wheels?"

"Yes," replied Cam. "We have towed it all the way from the United States so we could get right to work when we arrived."

"In that case," said the mayor, "you can park it under the tree at the far end of the square. You will be close to the public fountain, and you will have many villagers who will visit and help you to learn our language."

"Thank you," said Cam with genuine appreciation. "I look forward to getting to know you better."

Martin Méndez bowed slightly and stepped back, yelling something to the children as he did so.

The children scattered quickly as Cam guided the car and house trailer to their new home site at the far end of the town square. Soon he had the house trailer uncoupled and opened up. As he and Elvira and Evelyn arranged things inside, brown eyes stared in through the windows. *The mayor was right*, thought Cam. *There will be no shortage of visitors here.*

The house trailer became a continual source of entertainment for the village. Someone was always peering in to see what the "gringos" were doing inside. The Indians were particularly fascinated by teeth cleaning, something they had never seen before.

Life soon fell into a pattern for Cam, Elvira, and Evelyn. Elvira was still very weak and spent a good deal of her time lying in bed reading or sitting in the trailer writing letters. Evelyn took good care of her aunt. She also did the cooking and helped Cam in any way she could. The question of what to cook was a difficult one. The local Indians lived on a diet of tortillas, chilies, and a few beans. Meat consisted mainly of worms or tadpoles, which the locals ate either raw or fried. The two women could not bring themselves to eat the creatures, raw or fried, but Cam did so in an effort to make friends with the stall owners at the local market.

Cam decided one of his first jobs in Tetelcingo was to get to know the mayor, since he was the only person who could translate from Spanish into the Aztec language for him. The mayor was happy to be Cam's friend. Since Tetelcingo was very small, he often got bored and longed for outsiders to talk to. He came to visit Cam each morning after breakfast. At these meetings, Cam learned many things about Martin Méndez. The mayor was not a happy man. At different times over the past few years he had lived with twenty-eight women. Each woman had eventually left him because of his terrible temper. The mayor told Cam that he carried his pistol with him everywhere because he had made many enemies as a result of some unfair mayoral decisions.

Besides talking to and learning Aztec words from the mayor, each morning Cam read to him from a Spanish New Testament. Soon Martin Méndez asked Cam if he could have his own copy of the New Testament. Cam eagerly gave him one, and soon the mayor was reading it aloud from the steps of the municipal building. After he had read a passage in Spanish, he would translate it into Aztec so that those who had gathered to listen could get its meaning. Sometimes he read to the people in this way for two or three hours.

Several weeks after receiving his own Spanish New Testament, Martin Méndez came to speak to Cam. "Don Guillermo, something strange is happening to me. I cannot understand it. I can't do the things I used to do. I go to lie, and that book stops me. I can't even get drunk or beat up my woman anymore! You must tell me what is wrong."

Cam smiled. "You have read in the book how God can change people from the inside out. I think that is what is happening to you. Keep reading!"

A week later, Martin Méndez came to talk to Cam again. "This time I have put my gun away, don Guillermo. I do not want to wear it anymore, but I do want to buy three Bibles. I will send them to my enemies who want to kill me. I will write that this book has made me want to forgive them and that they should read it too and see if they can forgive me. I feel so different inside now, I no longer want to shoot people," he added.

This was even more than Cam had hoped for. The mayor becoming a Christian and reading and explaining the New Testament to the village each day was not something he had anticipated, at least not so soon.

Other noticeable improvements were happening in Tetelcingo. Cam, who had grown up on and around farms, could hardly believe the dull and unbalanced diet the Indians followed. He set about showing them how to grow a wide range of foods suited to their tropical climate. The town square was the perfect place to start, except for one thing. Over the years, all the good topsoil had been carted away to make adobe bricks. Cam set about inspiring the Indians to make new soil. Thousands of baskets of pig manure, bat dung, and ashes were spread over the square, and then Cam helped the Indians construct a simple irrigation system. With new "soil" and irrigation in place, Cam set off for Mexico City in his Buick to buy seed.

Cam returned with lettuce, carrot, celery, radish, and beet seeds. These were all plants the locals had never seen before. Rafael Ramírez also sent orange and lemon trees, and soon the village square was transformed into a lush garden. The people of the village loved to walk along the brick paths that crisscrossed the garden and ask the names of the various plants growing there. They would then try to imagine what the plant or its fruit might taste like.

When it was harvest time, Cam brought the schoolchildren out into the square. He showed them how to pull up the beets and cut the lettuce heads. Next he explained how the plants should be eaten. He then sent each child home with an armful of vegetables. Soon people were asking him how they could grow their own produce.

Cam knew that the Indians would need many things to grow their own vegetables, so he began making a list. As he listened to the needs of the people of the village, the list began to grow. Finally in October 1935, Cam was ready to go back to Mexico City and ask the government for: (1) Five hundred trees to plant along the streets, (2) a doctor to visit the village regularly and treat the poor free of charge, (3) cows, (4) timber to build public toilets, (5) money for the local store to expand the stock it carried, (6) pipes with which to construct a much larger irrigation system, and (7) publication of an Aztec-Spanish primer he had been working on so that people of all ages could learn to read their own language. Finally he added an eighth item to his wish list: a swimming pool for the children.

Once again Cam set off for Mexico City in his old Buick. He took with him many large heads of leafy green lettuce. He intended to present a head of lettuce to each person he met with. This was his way of showing them just what the Indians were capable of growing with a little help and knowledge.

In Mexico City, Cam met with many government officials. Each person Cam spoke to was very impressed. Although Cam didn't return with everything on his wish list, he did return with an old truck and a promise from Professor Zamora, the new director of rural education, that he would visit Tetelcingo to see for himself the progress being made there.

In early January 1936, an important visitor did come to Tetelcingo. Cam was weeding the garden in the village square when he heard the children start to shout, and it seemed like every dog in the area was barking. Cam wiped his hands on his coveralls and stepped out from behind a row of pole beans.

At the far end of the square, two large, black limousines, undoubtedly the first ever to enter the village, had pulled to a halt. A chauffeur jumped out of the lead car and opened the back door. A man in a dark suit stepped out. Cam stood in amazement. He immediately recognized the man as President Cárdenas.

Cam stood staring as the president shook hands with the village people who crowded around him. As he watched, Cam wondered what on earth the president of Mexico was doing in such a tiny, out-of-the-way place.

A few moments later, President Cárdenas's gaze fell on Cam. "Buenos días, señor presidente," Cam said as he stepped forward to shake the president's hand.

The president smiled. "Buenos días, señor Townsend," he replied.

The words whirled in Cam's head. Señor Townsend. The president knew his name!

"I have read about your good work," the president went on, "and I have come to inspect it for myself. First let me speak to the people."

At first Cam was too shocked to speak. Then he regained his composure. "Certainly, señor presidente. I would be honored if you would come to my humble trailer and see the work we are trying to do."

That is exactly what happened. After President Cárdenas had addressed the people of the village, he walked with Cam over to the house trailer, where the two of them sat together under the shade of a bamboo and cheesecloth awning. The president explained how he had been sent the Aztec reading primer Cam had prepared and had wanted the government to publish. This had led him to make inquiries about Cam's work. And the inquiries had brought the president to Tetelcingo to see firsthand what was being done for the Indians.

Cam was both honored to show his notes on the Aztec language to the president and surprised by the many questions the president asked about them. President Cárdenas asked questions only a translator would think to ask. Cam spoke of his desire to bring more translators into the country to start work on some of the other five hundred unwritten languages spoken in rural Mexico. After a while, the president began plying Cam with other questions. Who had made the garden outside? Would other translators make gardens, too?

Cam nodded. "Yes, señor presidente," he replied, "Each translator would come to your country to serve the people, just as Jesus came not to be served but to serve."

President Cárdenas looked impressed. "That is exactly what Mexico needs," he said, gently patting Cam on the shoulder. "Bring in all the translators you can get to come."

Long after the sleek, black limousines had disappeared down the dusty road, the president's words were still echoing through Cam's mind: *Bring in all the translators you can get to come.* That was exactly what Cam intended to do.

Chapter 15

Uncle Cam

It was July 1936, and Cameron Townsend surveyed the group of young people sitting in a semicircle around him. It was the first morning of the third Camp Wycliffe, and once again the camp was being held at Sulphur Springs, Arkansas. Eighteen students were seated on the nail kegs in front of Cam. Fourteen were enrolled as full-time attendees, and four were part-timers. Eunice Pike, a nurse, sat smiling between her brother Ken and the other single female student, Florence Hansen. Florence was a petite blonde who had recently graduated from the University of California at Los Angeles.

Cam didn't like to think about it, but he'd already had a disagreement with L.L. over having single female students. L.L. had been shocked when

Eunice and Florence applied for Camp Wycliffe. He had never for a moment considered that single women would respond to the call to live and work among remote Mexican tribes. In his mind it was a job for men, and he had wasted no time in telling Cam he should not accept female applicants. Cam, though, would not hear of it. After all, he pointed out, Camp Wycliffe was designed to weed out those who didn't have the stamina to survive in a primitive situation. He would wait until then to make a decision on the women, and he encouraged L.L. to do the same.

On the first day of camp, Cam told the students about the changes he had seen in Tetelcingo in the time he had been there. He showed them photos of Mayor Martin Méndez and told of how the mayor had come complaining to Cam that "the book" was stopping him from doing the bad things that up until then he had looked forward to doing. Cam also described the unexpected visit by President Lázaro Cárdenas and the president's invitation for Cam to bring as many translators as he could to Mexico. Last, he told them about all of the things that the president had done to help the Indians. A week after the president's visit, government trucks had begun rolling down the potholed road and into Tetelcingo. The first truck brought fruit trees, already in bud; the second carried a load of purebred pigs; and the third, a huge bull and a cow to improve the bloodline of the local cattle.

Cam explained how overwhelmed he was at President Cárdenas's personal interest in his project—interest that didn't stop with fruit trees and farm animals. There was much more. Several hundred acres of fertile land around Tetelcingo were purchased from Ladino landowners and given to the Indians so that they could grow their own crops. A small parcel of the land was set aside for a new school. Agronomists from the university in Mexico City were sent to help the Indians find better ways to grow crops, and a sprawling new irrigation system was dug. Simple land-tilling equipment was donated, along with a generator. Wires were strung to every house in the village so that the people could have electric lights in their homes.

Mrs. Cárdenas became interested, too. She sent clothes for the children and a sewing machine so that more could be made. A playground was built, and the government was even surveying a tract of land between Tetelcingo and the Pan American Highway so that a modern connecting road could be built. This would provide the Indians a way to get their new crops to market in Mexico City.

Everyone seated on the nail kegs around Cam cheered what was happening. It had been exactly a year since the students in the second Camp Wycliffe had prayed that God would change the hearts of those in the Mexican government. What a change they had seen in a year.

Camp Wycliffe went smoothly. This time instead of being a student, Ken Pike was one of the lecturers.

L.L. had his doubts about this. After all, Ken was only in his early twenties and looked even younger than that. But Cam saw tremendous potential in Ken Pike as a linguist and wanted to do all he could to encourage him. As it turned out, Ken was one of the most popular speakers, since he had firsthand stories about what life was like in a remote Mexican village. By the end of the camp, Ken had proved himself to be a knowledgeable and entertaining lecturer.

The two women students had shown as much ability during the camp as any of the men, and Cam could see no reason not to take them along on the trip south to Mexico. This time, though, Cam's niece Evelyn did not accompany them to Mexico. She went back to college to finish her degree, and her cousin, Ethel Mae Squires, took her place as Elvira's nurse and helper. By now, the young recruits in Camp Wycliffe had followed Evelyn and Ethel Mae's example and referred to Cameron Townsend as "Uncle Cam," a name that stuck. In the years to come, thousands of people all over the world would also refer to him that way.

Everyone was getting used to another name as well. Although Cam and the students and teachers in Camp Wycliffe called themselves Wycliffe Bible Translators, there were some problems with that name. Following Camp Wycliffe the year before, Bill Sedat had encountered a lot of difficulty getting into Guatemala. Immigration officials at the border had wanted to know what educational institution was sponsoring him. They cared little that he was a Wycliffe Bible translator. They wanted a letter of recommendation on official letterhead from the sponsoring institution. Of course, there was none, and when Bill wrote to Cam about the situation, it got Cam thinking about how to deal with it. By the time the third Camp Wycliffe had rolled around, Cam had come up with a plan. It was time to form their own sponsoring institution. Indeed, Cam was aware that many of his contacts in foreign countries were a result of his linguistics work and not his missionary work, though in his mind they were one and the same. Consequently, he had come up with the name Summer Institute of Linguistics. The name sounded official, and the students liked it. And so SIL, as the name was quickly shortened to, was born.

The new organization needed a committee to run it, and so Ken Pike, Brainerd Legters, and Max Lathrop, students from the previous Camp Wycliffe, along with Eugene Nida, a student in the present school, were chosen to form the committee. Cam, of course, was given the position of director, but he insisted the rules of the new organization be written in such a way that as director he did not have the final say in any decision. He insisted the committee have that say. Most people had never heard of such a thing. A director should direct, many of Cam's friends told him. But Cam was insistent. He did not want SIL to be a "one-man band." He said everyone in the organization was expected to work hard, and everyone should have a voice in what happened.

In the fall of 1936, two carloads of would-be Bible translators drove into Mexico City, where Cam had rented an apartment for them. The day after their arrival, an official government car pulled up in front of their apartment house, and a courier climbed out. He carried with him an invitation from President Cárdenas. Cam tore open the envelope and read the card inside. The president had heard that Cam and a new group of translators were in town, and he was going to host a banquet in their honor. The banquet would commence at three o'clock that afternoon.

The group erupted into a flurry of activity. Best clothes had to be unpacked and ironed, and Elvira gave a crash course in how to behave around the president of Mexico. By two-thirty Cam, Elvira, Ethel Mae, and the ten young translators were ready and waiting as the enormous presidential limousine pulled up to the curb. Colonel Beteta, the president's chief of staff, stepped out and greeted the group before they all piled into the car.

The limousine wound its way through the back streets of Mexico City and on up into the foothills surrounding the city. The car climbed steadily until they arrived at Chapultepec Castle, the magnificent home of the French Emperor Maximilian. Colonel Beteta took them on a guided tour of the castle while they waited to be summoned for the banquet.

Finally, a bell sounded, and Cam led the group into the ancient dining hall where kings and princes had dined in times past. Standing at the head of a long carved table was President Cárdenas. He reached out and embraced Cam like a long-lost brother. Cam greeted the president warmly and asked if he could introduce his group of translators. One by one, the translators stepped forward and shook hands with President Cárdenas. Next the president introduced the government officials he had invited to meet the group: the governor of the state of Michoacán, the governor of the state of Quintana Roo, and the undersecretary of foreign affairs.

Once the introductions were over, the president invited everyone to be seated, with Cam on his right and Elvira on his left. The nine-course dinner took two hours to serve. President Cárdenas talked to Cam nearly the whole time, asking questions about the various students and what they hoped to achieve in Mexico. Cam answered honestly, as he always did, explaining that they had come to do translation work that would eventually lead to translating the Bible. He pointed out that the students would also do whatever they could to improve the lives of the Indians they worked among.

Every so often Cam looked down the long, flower-decorated table at his new recruits. He wondered whether the president would notice just how much they were eating! After surviving on a diet of fruit, milkshakes, and bread on their journey down, many of them were ready for a good meal. And the courses kept coming, along with President Cárdenas's questions.

Near the end of the meal, the president leaned over to Cam. "My government will do everything it can to help you," he said. He then glanced at Walter Miller, the skinniest of Cam's students, and asked Cam, "Do they have enough money to live in Mexico?"

Cam hesitated for a moment. He could not tell a lie, but he hoped the truth would not put their mission in jeopardy. "Two of them have been promised support from friends and family back home, but not the other eight," he said.

President Cárdenas's eyes lit up. "Well, in that case, there is something we can do to help right away. I will arrange for the others to be paid as if they were rural schoolteachers."

Cam was speechless. If there had been any doubt the president was behind the work of SIL, it was swept away at that moment.

"And," President Cárdenas continued, "my wife is greatly interested in your work, though she could not attend the banquet tonight. She would like it very much if your wife and the two charming young ladies in your group would pay her a visit. I will send my car for them, of course."

"Gracias, señor presidente," replied Cam. "You have done so much for us. We will work hard to be worthy of the trust you have placed in us."

It was after seven when Colonel Beteta finally escorted them all back to their apartment. When they got there, they sat around too full to move, except for Cam, who had spent so much time talking that he had eaten almost nothing at all. Cam related to the students the wonderful offer the president had made, and everyone was excited. Now everything was in place, and soon it would be time to spread out around the countryside.

There was growing concern for the two single women, however. The women hoped to go to the remote mountain village of Mazatec in Oaxaca, but when other missionaries in Mexico City learned of the plan, they were horrified. Norman Taylor, a veteran missionary in Mexico, visited Cam and urged him to reconsider sending the two women to Mazatec. To him it was inconceivable that two single women in their early twenties with no experience would be sent to an area where no male missionaries had ever settled. Norman had been through the area once himself and reported that there was a high rate of murder in the province. Cam was almost swayed by his argument, until he talked to Eunice Pike and Florence Hansen. The women were both surprised that Cam was having second thoughts about sending them to Mazatec. "But Uncle Cam," Florence asked, "don't you believe God will take care of us?"

Cam had no answer to their query. "Well, if you put it that way," he said, "go right ahead."

And so they did. Ken Pike escorted his sister Eunice and Florence Hansen to their outpost. In the meantime, Brainerd Legters and his new wife, Elva, headed for the Maya tribe on the Yucatan peninsula. Walter and Vera Miller took a train to Oaxaca to work among the Mixe tribe, and Richmond McKinney chose the Otomis tribe in the Mesquital Valley to work amongst. Eugene Nida took a bus into the Madre Mountains to work with the Tarahumara tribe, and Landis Christiansen hiked into the steep Puebla Mountains to work with the Totonacs.

Once the students had departed, the Townsends, accompanied by Ethel Mae Squires, headed back to Tetelcingo, where for the next several years Cam continued his translation and community work.

Chapter 16

New Recruits

It was October 1941, and Cam and Elvira were visiting the Lathrops, who lived in a house on the edge of Lake Pátzcuaro about two hundred miles west of Mexico City. As usual, Cam rose early in the morning to read his Bible. It was a picture-perfect morning. As the sun rose over the lake, Tarascan fishermen paddled their canoes out from the shore and threw their nets into the deep blue water. From his seat on the porch, the scene reminded Cam of the verses he had just read in the Gospel of Matthew, chapter 4, where, as Jesus watched the fishermen on the Lake of Galilee, He turned to His disciples and said, "Follow me and I will make you fishers of men." Something stirred deep within Cam as he thought of the millions of people who still did not have one word of Scripture written in their own language. He wondered how these people could possibly follow Jesus if they didn't get to hear or read about His invitation.

As he sat watching the fishermen rhythmically pulling in their catch, Cam somehow knew it was time to redouble his efforts. He reached for a piece of paper and began drafting a letter to the forty-four Wycliffe workers who were now spread out across Mexico. "Will each of you be responsible before the Lord for one new Bible translation?" he wrote. He then went on to tell them of his goal of recruiting fifty more workers within a year.

When he was finished writing, Cam went inside to tell Elvira about his new goal. As usual, she brought him back to reality with questions. Where would the recruits get their support money? Who would process it for them? And where would they train? The tiny camp in the Ozark Mountains could not fit that many people for training.

Cam agreed that the questions were good ones. He decided that the best thing to do was to take a trip back to the United States to get things in order for the fifty new recruits he was believing would join SIL that year. It was an ideal time to take a break from Mexico. Dick and Karen Pittman were now in Tetelcingo carrying on the translation work Cam had begun. And the work in Mexico was progressing well. Indeed, just days before, Cam had hosted a banquet in Mexico City to honor five years of cooperation between SIL, the Ministry of

Education, and the National University. Elena Trejo, the young Guatemalan girl who, along with Joe Chicol, Cam and Elvira had taken into their home to live, was the speaker. She was grown up now, of course, but she had made the most of the education the Townsends had offered her when they sent her to California to live with Cam's parents so that she could attend high school. She had gone to medical school from there and had become a skilled surgeon. Finally, she had returned to Guatemala, where she was the first woman doctor in the entire country. Cam invited her to speak and tell those at the banquet how educational opportunities had opened up a whole new area of opportunity for her. Elena gave a fine speech, and Cam was very proud of her.

Two years before, Cam's father had died, and five months after that, L.L. also died unexpectedly. As a result, Cam was anxious to visit his sisters and other friends back home.

Cam and Elvira crossed the border back into the United States just as Japan was bombing Pearl Harbor, thrusting the country into the Second World War. Some of the people Cam stayed with doubted he would find his fifty new recruits now that the government was busy drafting so many men into the war effort. Cam, though, was undeterred. He remembered how twenty-four years before his captain had signed his release from the draft. He was sure that war would not stand in the way of Bible translation.

In Los Angeles, Cam and Elvira stayed with Will Nyman, their faithful supporter who had hosted the two students from the first Camp Wycliffe. Will had a gift for organizing, and he agreed to take over the administration work that L.L. had been doing for Wycliffe Bible Translators. Cam still believed there would soon be fifty new recruits arriving, and there was more need than ever for a team of people in the United States who could arrange visas, send out newsletters, and process support money for those translating the Bible out on the mission field. Will plunged into the job with his usual enthusiasm. He converted the room above his garage into an office, and soon things were running more smoothly than ever before.

From Los Angeles, Cam and Elvira made their way to the University of Oklahoma. The year before, Della Brunstetter, a French teacher at the university with an interest in the Cherokee language, had attended Camp Wycliffe. She had heard about the camp's lively teachers and their methods for quick and reliable results in the field. Della had been more impressed by the program than she had expected, so impressed that she went back to the University of Oklahoma and requested a meeting with the board of regents. At the meeting she suggested the university allow Camp Wycliffe to use the facilities for its summer linguistics camps. Furthermore, because the school was of such a high standard, she also suggested the college give Camp Wycliffe full academic credit. The Board of Regents studied the idea and agreed to the request. Cam came to Oklahoma to meet with the board, and soon afterwards a formal invitation was issued for Camp Wycliffe to be held at the University of Oklahoma campus in 1942.

Cam was overjoyed with this unexpected new development, as well as with the news that Ken Pike was negotiating with Briercrest Bible School in Canada to hold a Camp Wycliffe there. Max Lathrop was busy, too. He had started a magazine called *Translation* to keep the public up-to-date with information on the work of SIL.

The applications for Camp Wycliffe began to flow in until 130 young people had signed up for the school. Indeed, the summer of 1942 Camp Wycliffe turned out to be the best ever. That fall, at the end of the school, fifty-one of the students set out to work among various Indian tribes in Mexico. Cam was elated. Despite the war, God had given him the fifty recruits he'd asked for, and one more!

Cam and Elvira continued touring the United States, speaking publicly and privately to anyone who would listen to what they had to say about linguistics and Bible translation. They also spent a number of weeks helping Will Nyman, since there was more work than ever to do now that they had an additional fifty-one workers in the field.

Doors of opportunity seemed to be swinging open everywhere. Ken Pike, who now had his Ph.D. in linguistics, visited Peru and wrote that the government there had invited SIL to begin working among the Indian tribes of the Amazon jungle. And three translators who were working among the Navajo Indians joined SIL, making them the organization's first translators outside Mexico. This pleased Cam greatly. He was concerned at the way Native American Indian speakers had been neglected by linguists even though they were within the borders of the United States.

With 103 workers fanned out across Mexico, Mexico City became a hub of activity for SIL. There was always someone passing through the capital on his or her way home or to a new assignment. Cam decided it was time the organization purchased its own building. He found an old boarding house that had once been used for tourists. The house had twenty-five rooms, which seemed a lot of rooms at first, but within months the rooms had been converted into guest bedrooms, offices, and a room for the printing press. The place was soon dubbed "The Kettle" by SIL workers because it was always "boiling over" with workers and activity.

While back in Mexico, Cam had another of his "bright ideas." Over the years, he and Elvira had become close friends of President Lázaro Cárdenas and his wife, Amalia. Cam greatly admired the way the president had tried to improve the living conditions of the lowest classes of Mexican society. He believed that such a great man should have a biography written about him to be an example to other leaders. Cam decided to write the book himself.

Several years before, Al Johnson, the retired president of National Life Insurance Company, had invited Cam and Elvira to stay at his home in Hollywood whenever they needed a break. By November 1944, Cam had gathered all the material he needed to begin writing the biography of President Cárdenas. He decided to take Al up on his offer, as it seemed the perfect place to get away and write.

Cam was right. The house in Hollywood was a perfect place to write. All was going well until the evening of December 23, 1944. Cam had just climbed into bed when Elvira began clutching her chest. "There's no air," she gasped, ripping back the sheets and groping her way to the window.

Cam rushed after Elvira. As he reached her, she collapsed into his arms. He carried her back to bed and called for Al to help him. Elvira lay still all night, gasping for every breath she took. The doctor came, but there was nothing he could do except suggest that Cam keep her as comfortable as possible. And that is what Cam did. He sat by the bed holding his wife's hand and praying with her hour after hour. Finally, on Christmas Eve, Elvira's breathing became shallower, until she stopped breathing altogether.

Cam sat stunned. He had seen Elvira near death so many times before, but somehow she had always managed to pull herself back from the brink. This time there was no coming back. Fifty-two-year-old Elvira Townsend was dead. Half an hour later, Al gently led Cam from the room as he struggled to come to terms with his wife's death.

Al Johnson generously paid for a large funeral that was held in nearby Glendale, California. Cam was too broken-hearted to trust himself to speak at the funeral, so he wrote a short piece for his friend Dawson Trotman to read during the service. It began: "God gave Elvira as a love gift to the people of Latin America and to us. He used her by His power and now He has taken His handiwork to Himself. The task she served, however, remains, and we remain."

Elvira Townsend's gravesite was not like any other. Rather than have people give the traditional flowers, Cam had asked them to purchase Spanish New Testaments for distribution in Mexico and Guatemala. Stacked neatly around Elvira's grave were thousands of New Testaments that Cam would personally see were put to good use in Latin America.

Following Elvira's death, Cam threw himself into planning SIL's new translation work in Peru. He visited the country, flying over the Andes Mountains and into the mighty Amazon Basin, where he met with the few missionaries dotted along the streams and tributaries that eventually flowed into the largest river on earth. Cam was greatly challenged by the work that needed to be done in Peru. Many of the Indian tribes had little or no contact with the outside world. Their lives were shrouded in witch doctor curses and revenge killings.

The more time Cam spent in the Amazon jungle, the more he prayed for two things: medical people to work alongside the translators, and airplanes and pilots to quickly and safely transport the missionaries in and out of the jungle. The alternative to flying was days, even weeks, of tedious hiking, often into areas without the slightest hint of a trail.

Not too long after Elvira's death, Cam decided to head back to the United States via Mexico. He planned to speak in churches about SIL's needs in Peru and to look for airplanes, along with pilots and doctors who could form a core team of workers in Peru.

While in Mexico, Cam visited Tetelcingo, as he always tried to do when he was visiting the country. He had so many friends there, and the Indians were anxious to comfort him after hearing of Elvira's death. Cam's spirits were buoyed by what he saw. Several SIL families were now living there, along with Elaine Miekle, a tall, blue-eyed teacher from Chicago who was SIL's first support worker. Elaine's job was to teach the three school-aged children of the Wycliffe translators. Cam liked Elaine immediately and soon learned how overqualified she was for the job. Before joining Wycliffe, Elaine had been the supervisor of special education for over three hundred schools in Chicago. At twenty-six, she had been the youngest supervisor ever appointed to the school district. Cam was impressed at the way she had given it all up to come and teach three students in a makeshift hut with a leaky roof. Cam and Elaine became good friends, and when

Cam had to leave for the United States, they agreed to write to each other.

Back in Los Angeles, Cam visited Dawson Trotman at his office. Dawson Trotman was the founder of the Navigators, an organization that reached out with the gospel to young people in the military. During their conversation, Cam learned that until just a few days before, a fledgling ministry called CAMF (Christian Airmen's Missionary Fellowship) had been sharing a corner of Dawson's office. Since the Navigators had needed the office space back, Betty Greene, the cofounder of the group, had moved to a new office downtown.

Cam could hardly believe what he was hearing. One of the reasons he was back in the United States was to recruit pilots for the new SIL work in Peru, and here he was hearing about an entire organization of Christian pilots. Cam plied Dawson with all sorts of questions about Betty Greene and her organization. He soon learned that Betty had been a member of the WASP, the Women Airforce Service Pilots. The WASPs didn't fly combat missions, but they played an important role in ferrying airplanes to their destinations and flying planes used in war practice. Now that the war was in its final stages, the WASP was being disbanded, and Betty had taken up the challenge of becoming the first full-time member of CAMF. The goal of the organization was to provide airplanes and pilots to help missionaries do their work faster and more safely. It was exactly the same goal as Cam's! Apparently,

Betty Greene had been swamped by hundreds of letters a month from men who had been trained as pilots and aircraft mechanics for the war and were now wondering whether their new skills could be put to use in Christian service once the war was over. Of course, the one problem the new organization had was that it didn't have any airplanes for these pilots to fly.

Cam very much wanted to meet Betty Greene and tell her about SIL's plans to use airplanes to transport missionaries in Peru, but right then he had to travel across the country to fulfill some speaking obligations. He made a note to tell Will Nyman to contact Betty and set up a meeting between her and Cam in the near future.

Cam had a feeling things were going to work out so that the two organizations could work together. In the meantime, there was something he could do to help CAMF. He placed a phone call to Pastor Erickson, a pastor in Chicago and supporter of the work of SIL. "I think I have a pilot," he said. "All she needs is an airplane to fly. Would your church be able to raise $2,500 to help buy one?"

Chapter 17

Jungle Camp

Cam stood at the train station in Chicago stretch-ing his neck for a glimpse of Elaine Miekle. He hoped he'd done the right thing coming to meet her. It had been a spur-of-the-moment decision. He had been at Briercrest Bible College looking in on the Canadian Camp Wycliffe when he received the message that Elaine's grandmother had died and Elaine was on her way back to Chicago for the funeral. Cam's first thought had been to phone Elaine and tell her how sorry he was at the news, but then he remembered that he had asked Pastor Erickson to ask his church to help buy an airplane for Peru. Suddenly it had occurred to him that he could take the train to Chicago and visit both Elaine Miekle and Pastor Erickson in one trip.

181

A minute later, Cam spotted Elaine's curly hair through the jostling crowd. He waved enthusiastically, and when Elaine saw him, she waved back. Soon Cam was being introduced to Elaine's father. He was taken aback by Mr. Miekle. Cam was forty-nine years old, and Mr. Miekle was only ten years older than he was. Cam began wondering what Mr. Miekle would think if he knew Cam was interested in his thirty-year-old daughter. Such thoughts were soon forgotten, however, as Elaine and Cam were whisked off by car through the streets of Chicago. They had so much to tell each other. Cam wanted to know all about the work in Tetelcingo, and Elaine was excited to hear how he may have found his first pilot. She was also happy to hear that Dr. Ken Altig, a medical doctor and Camp Wycliffe graduate, was seriously considering joining the team for Peru.

The days passed quickly. Cam divided his time between Pastor Erickson and his Gospel Tabernacle congregation, and Elaine Miekle and her family. Cam and Elaine enjoyed every minute they spent together, and by the time Elaine was ready to return to Mexico, the two of them were in love. Cam wasted no time in asking Mr. Miekle if he could marry Elaine. Mr. Miekle agreed heartily, as long as that was what Elaine wanted. It was, and the two parted promising to write to each other every day until Cam had finished his work in the United States and could return to Mexico.

Cam had a lot to do. He had kept in touch with Ken Pike, who was running Camp Wycliffe at the

University of Oklahoma. Ken reported that seventeen men and six women, all of them single, had
signed up to go to Peru. The number greatly pleased
Cam. World War II had ended with Japan's formal
surrender aboard the USS *Missouri* in Tokyo Bay on
September 2, 1945, and Cam expected an upsurge in
recruits as young Christian service men and women
looked for new challenges. Indeed, Cam had
already decided that these new recruits would need
extra training in jungle survival and had set about
planning a jungle camp in Mexico.

On his way back to Mexico in September 1945 to
prepare the site for the jungle camp, Cam stopped
in Los Angeles to visit Dawson Trotman. He told
Dawson how Will Nyman had been in touch with
CAMF and how the group was very interested in
providing pilots and airplanes to meet the needs of
SIL translators. Indeed, CAMF had located a Waco
biplane for sale that would be perfect for the job.
The owner wanted five thousand dollars for it, and
through the generosity of Pastor Erickson's congregation, Wycliffe Bible Translators had been able to
give half the money toward the purchase of the
plane. It was hoped that the plane would soon be
overhauled and then flown to Mexico, where it
would be based. Cam also told Dawson about Ken
Altig's decision to go to Peru and that Elaine had
said yes to his marriage proposal.

Everything was in place when the twenty-three-
member team of translators bound for Peru arrived
at the jungle camp near Tuxtla, the capital of the

state of Chiapas in southern Mexico. Al Johnson, Cam's old friend, had generously chartered an airplane to carry the SIL workers to the site, since the Waco biplane was not yet ready. The three-month camp was unlike anything the young Americans had ever experienced. It was one long test of survival. The students paddled heavily laden canoes through white-water rapids, hiked over rough mountain passes, hunted for food, constructed makeshift huts without tools, and learned how to treat snakebites and use penicillin, the newest drug on the market. And, of course, they did all this while continuing with their linguistics studies.

At the end of three months, all twenty-three students were ready and eager to begin work in Peru. Cam was eager to get to Peru, too—he just had a wedding to plan first. Originally, Cam had decided that he and Elaine should have an engagement of three years. He planned to wait until the work in Peru was well under way, but his friends urged him not to wait. They pointed out that he and Elaine were obviously a happy couple and there seemed no point in delaying the wedding. Elaine would fit in as easily in Peru as she had in Mexico.

Cam asked Lázaro Cárdenas, the now-retired president of Mexico, to be his best man, and Elaine asked Amalia Cárdenas to be her matron of honor. The Cárdenases gladly agreed and insisted that the wedding be held at their beautiful home on the shores of Lake Pátzcuaro, about a ten-hour drive west of Mexico City. Cam kept the guest list small, or as small as he could, but because of his work with government officials, many important people had to be invited. The wedding was held on April 4, 1946, and the ceremony and reception went off without a hitch, complete with an orchestra, a wedding gift from the Cárdenases.

Cam and Elaine honeymooned nearby for two days before getting back to work. They had bags and barrels to pack, as all their belongings were gathered up to be sent to Peru. On the way to Peru, Cam and Elaine planned to travel through Venezuela, where Cam had arranged meetings with the Venezuelan president and members of his cabinet to discuss SIL's eventually moving into the tribal areas of the country to do translation work.

After the trip to Venezuela, Cam and Elaine were reunited with the team in an old, unfurnished house in the poor sector of Lima, Peru. Soon afterwards, the person handling the finances for the group confided in Cam that somehow the money had been counted wrong in Mexico City. Instead of there being enough to cover the group's cost for the first three months in Peru, there was barely enough money to cover a month's expenses, and it was going fast. Cam gave an understanding nod. By now he knew that things seldom turned out to be as easy as they had first seemed. He talked to Elaine about the situation, and she agreed they should give their wedding gifts, totaling eleven hundred dollars in cash, to help make up the difference. That amount, along with an unexpected gift of five hundred dollars from Cam's home church in Los Angeles, was enough to pay the rent and buy food for the group.

Before long, the team of translators was scattered in pairs throughout the Peruvian jungle. Cam and Elaine set up home in the jungle at a site that overlooked the Aguaytia River. The site was also situated on the main highway from Lima and was to be SIL's base camp in Peru. Elaine was pleased to have a hut to call her own, especially since she had just learned she was pregnant; the baby was due sometime in January 1947.

The baby, a six-pound girl whom they named Grace, was born early, two days after Christmas. At the age of fifty, Cam was a dad for the first time, and he couldn't have been happier about it! Little Gracie, as she soon became known, was a traveler almost from the start. She was only six weeks old when she flew with her parents to the jungle camp near Tuxtla, Mexico, where a second group of recruits was waiting to be trained to go into the jungle. The second jungle camp was even more successful than the first, because Cam and Elaine had a lot more firsthand knowledge to share, since they now lived in the jungle themselves.

Time at the jungle camp passed quickly, and soon the Townsends were ready to head back to Peru. Cam helped Elaine climb into the back seat of the Piper Super Cruiser airplane and then handed in baby Gracie, sound asleep in the woven basket she used as a bed. Neatly folded beneath her was a batch of freshly dried diapers, ready for the trip. Cam waved one last time to the students as he swung himself into the seat beside his wife. He adjusted Gracie's basket so that it lay evenly over both of their laps.

Since Betty Greene was busy flying some missionaries to another location in the Waco biplane, a commercial pilot and plane had flown in to pick the Townsends up. The pilot checked his gauges before cranking the Piper's engine to life. He turned the plane around, set the flaps for takeoff, and gunned the engine. Soon the Piper Super Cruiser was barreling down the rough, doglegged airstrip. They were about three-quarters of the way down the airstrip when the wheels lifted off the ground. Cam reached over and squeezed Elaine's hand. "We'll be in Tuxtla in no time," he said.

Both of them turned to take one last look at the students, still waving from the far end of the airstrip. As Cam looked back he knew something was wrong. The plane was so close to the trees he could hear their branches scraping against the undercarriage. And the pilot seemed to be wrestling with the control stick. Suddenly there was a tearing sound, and Cam felt the plane nosedive. He barely had time to shield Gracie with his body before the plane crashed against the side of a ravine, bounced twice, and landed on its side against a tree.

Cam lay in the wreckage, his left leg pinned under him. The smell of airplane fuel filled the air as he cautiously turned his head to check on his family. A surge of relief rushed through him when Gracie let out a loud scream and Elaine moved her head. Cam heard tapping on the window, and he turned to see an Indian man peering in at them.

By now fuel was pouring into the airplane, and Cam's only thought was fire. Blood was gushing from his left hip, and Elaine's foot was trapped, but the baby was free. Quickly, Cam grabbed Gracie, bundled her in the spare diapers, opened the window, and handed Gracie to the man. "Run!" he yelled in Spanish, "Run! Fire, fire!"

Terror was reflected in the Indian man's eyes as he took Gracie and leapt away from the plane.

With Gracie safe, Cam knew the rest of them had to get out of the plane as soon as possible. He reached over and shook the pilot, who groaned but did not move. Cam could see that the pilot's head was pinned against the control panel. He then turned his attention to his wife.

"It's my ankle," Elaine moaned.

Cam looked down. Elaine's foot hung loosely at the end of her leg like that of a puppet. "Come on," he urged, as much for his own benefit as for hers. "We have to get ourselves out of here now. I'll help you."

Painfully the two of them crawled out the window of the crashed airplane and fell clumsily onto the ground.

About then, several of the jungle camp students arrived on the scene. A few moments later, Dr. Culley, who was working with the students, also arrived. Together they pulled the pilot from the wreckage and tore up clothing for bandages to bind the wounds on Cam's leg and Elaine's ankle. Minutes later, more students arrived with blankets, and makeshift stretchers were made from some sturdy tree branches.

Cam was conscious the whole time, and his mind was racing. He wished the folks back home could see how unreliable commercial flights could be in the jungle. Maybe then they would fund more airplanes and experienced pilots for SIL. Suddenly, ignoring the throbbing pain in his crushed leg, Cam had an idea. "Dale," he yelled to one of the students. "Go and get the movie camera and film us and the wreckage before we're moved. People back home need to see this!"

Dale Kietzman looked stunned for a moment, and then he sprinted off to do as Cam had asked. Within minutes, the footage was shot, and the three injured people were lifted up the side of the ravine and taken back to one of the huts at the jungle camp. Dr. Culley tended to their wounds as best he could, and he was very relieved when a radio call to President Cárdenas produced another doctor, a nursing assistant, and an array of bandages and drugs to treat the patients.

It was twelve days before either doctor felt that the three injured patients were stable enough to be transferred to a hospital in Mexico City. Little Gracie, who was unharmed by the accident, stayed behind to be looked after by the students and teachers at the jungle camp.

Once they were relocated to a hospital, both Cam and Elaine had surgery to repair their injured legs. Cam's thigh was so badly injured that a metal plate had to be permanently inserted to add extra support. And Elaine's ankle required major reconstructive surgery. As a result, Elaine was unable to walk without the aid of crutches for six months, and the injury was to bother her for the rest of her life.

Despite the pain Cam and Elaine endured, two good things did come out of the plane crash. First, Cam stayed still long enough to complete *Lázaro Cárdenas, Mexican Democrat,* the biography of the president he had been working on for years. Second, Cam realized that SIL needed to have its own airplane service in the jungle. CAMF and Betty Greene had been very helpful, but there was no way Betty's organization would be able to grow fast enough to cover all SIL's needs. Even though SIL funds had dropped to an all-time low, Cam began making notes on exactly how a jungle aviation service should operate.

As soon as he was well enough, Cam went to the United States, where a SIL board meeting was being held. Many encouraging things were shared at the meeting. Ken Pike was preparing to start a Camp Wycliffe in Australia to train linguists to translate the Bible into the many aboriginal languages spoken in Australia. And nearby New Guinea had entered the world's spotlight during World War II. No one knew how many languages were spoken in the mist-shrouded highland areas of the island. Few white people had set foot in the thousands of square miles of mountainous interior.

When Cam introduced his idea for an aviation department, the atmosphere in the room turned glum. No one had much enthusiasm for the project. The other six members of the board argued that it would cost an enormous amount of money to set it up and just as much to keep it running. Besides, it was hard for them to see just what business missionaries had with airplanes.

Cam reasoned with the board members. He told them that in his view, being in the jungle meant they were in aviation whether they liked it or not. In the end, Cam did not manage to bring the group around to his point of view, but he did get them to agree that the project could go ahead on one condition: Forty thousand dollars had to be in the bank for the project by the next board meeting, scheduled for 1949.

Chapter 18

The Pavilion

Cameron Townsend had no doubt that God wanted SIL involved in aviation. Everywhere he went he enthusiastically spoke about his vision of having airplanes ferrying Wycliffe Bible translators in and out of the jungle all over the world. Soon others began to embrace the vision, too. A small committee was set up to oversee the project, and money began to trickle in. A grocer in San Diego, California, donated a small airplane that was sold and the money put away in a designated bank account to buy bigger, more useful aircraft.

Even after he returned to Peru to continue his work there, Cam was constantly writing letters to people and explaining the need for reliable transportation for SIL missionaries. Just to underscore the point he was making, into each letter he would tuck a few photographs of him and Elaine in the hospital after the plane crash.

Besides letter writing, the Townsends had a lot to keep them busy. They built a new hut for the three of them to live in, and then they added an extra room when they found out Elaine was expecting a baby due in May 1948. Cam and Elaine named their second daughter Joy.

The Townsends did not have much money to buy building materials, and Cam did the best he could with what he had. He nailed together a wooden frame for the roof and walls, and Elaine sewed together some sheets of canvas fabric which were then pulled over the frame to form a roof and walls. Although the hut looked like a big tent, it was Cam and Elaine's first home, and they loved it, at least until the rainy season came. During the rainy season, the hut became unbearably hot inside, and the bugs seemed to fight each other to get inside!

By September 1949, the work of SIL in Peru was progressing well, especially since the organization had added its first shortwave radio transmitter and receiver. The radio helped the Wycliffe translators keep in touch with each other, and with Dr. Altig when emergencies arose. The usefulness of the shortwave radio made Cam even more determined to work towards using airplanes on the mission field.

Towards the end of September, Cam flew to Oklahoma for the scheduled SIL board meeting. When he arrived, he found $41,000 waiting in the account to be used to buy and maintain airplanes. Cam had met the goal set at the previous board meeting, with a thousand dollars to spare. As a result, it was agreed that Jungle Aviation and Radio Service, or JAARS for short, should be established. Cam was elated by the result of the meeting.

Cam arrived back home in Peru just in time for the birth of his third child, another daughter, whom they named Elainadel. The baby was born on December 28, 1949, the day after her sister Grace's third birthday. Elaine now had her hands full.

While Cam was delighted at the arrival of his new daughter, he had something else on his mind. He was thinking about the movie he had encouraged SIL to make about the need for Bible translators and the work they were doing. Irwin Moon, a top documentary maker of the time, had offered his time free of charge and filmed the necessary footage for the project. Now all the pieces needed to be edited into a documentary. It was a long and detailed job, and SIL could not afford to pay anyone to do it. Cam could not bear to think of the rolls of film sitting in a vault somewhere. Since no one could be found to edit the film, Cam decided to do it himself. The five members of the Townsend family packed their bags and headed for the Moody Institute of Science Studios near Los Angeles. Irwin Moon had obtained permission from the institute for Cam to use its state-of-the-art editing suite. Cam set to work while Elaine handled the correspondence and watched over their three very active little girls.

Five months later, in July 1950, Cam finally finished the film to his high standard. The documentary was titled, *Oh for a Thousand Tongues*, and it was an instant hit. Charles Fuller, the famous radio host, introduced the work of SIL, and Cam narrated the film himself. Many people declared it to be the best Christian film they had ever seen. Once more, Cameron Townsend had found an effective way to help people understand the need for Bible translation around the world.

On subsequent visits to the United States, Cam often showed the film in the churches he visited. After the film had been shown, he would always wrap up with his favorite challenge: "The greatest missionary of all is the Bible in a person's own language. It never needs a furlough, and it is never considered a foreigner."

The work of Wycliffe Bible Translators, as SIL was alternately known in North America, continued to grow over the next few years. New translation projects were begun in the Philippines, and young men and women from many countries, including New Zealand, Australia, Sweden, and the United Kingdom, joined the organization. One by one, airplanes and pilots were being added, until by Christmas 1950, JAARS had four airplanes that were being used to transport and service the 280 full-time SIL workers spread around the world.

Cam and Elaine had one more child. The baby was born on January 20, 1953, and this time it was a boy. They named him William, and called him Billy for short.

Everything seemed to be going well. SIL was growing, partly because of the impact the *Oh for a Thousand Tongues* documentary had on the people who watched it. However, it wasn't until 1962, nine years after Billy was born, that Cam began thinking about his biggest publicity plan yet. Cam was visiting JAARS headquarters in Charlotte, North Carolina, when a public relations man visited him. Cam told the man several stories about what was happening with SIL in Latin America.

The man's eyes lit up. "Wow!" he exclaimed, "That is amazing. Why don't more people know about your organization?"

"Well," replied Cam, "we get the word out whenever we can. There's a documentary out about our work, and a new book called *One Thousand Tongues to Go* has recently been published."

"Good," replied the man. "But you need more. You need a way to get millions of Americans to hear about your ideas. Think of the new workers you could attract!"

"I agree," said Cam. "But what more can we do?"

The man's face lit up. "I've got just the thing. Why don't you set up a pavilion at the New York World's Fair? It's in 1964, but they are already accepting applications for pavilions. In fact, I have a friend who is on the fair's committee." The man reached into his pocket and pulled out a business card. "Here," he said, handing the card to Cam. "This man should be able to give you all the information you need. Tell him I gave you his name."

After the man left, Cam sat at his desk with the business card in front of him. Was it possible for Wycliffe Bible Translators to have its own pavilion at the World's Fair? It was a great idea, since not just Americans but people from all over the world would be there. Cam wondered how much such a pavilion would cost and who would run it.

A week later, Cam had an answer to the first question. A site for the smallest pavilion at the New York World's Fair cost a quarter of a million dollars! Cam checked his bank account; it had exactly two hundred fifty dollars in it. Having a pavilion at the World's Fair may have sounded like a wonderful idea, but it wasn't practical, at least not right then. Still, who knew what might happen next, Cam told himself as he tucked the business card away in his file cabinet. He would just wait and see.

In the meantime, Cam had plenty to keep him busy. SIL now had over fifteen hundred workers fanned out around the world, and Cam tried to keep in personal touch with as many of them as possible.

In February 1963, Cam attended another SIL board meeting in Mexico City. He mentioned the idea of a pavilion at the New York World's Fair, but the board didn't have much enthusiasm to discuss the matter further. Such a pavilion would cost more money than the organization could ever hope to see in ten years.

Cam, though, did not forget the idea. He just stored it away as the board members went on to discuss other business. New teams of translators were setting up in Nigeria and Ghana in Africa, and someone raised the issue of how computers might help speed up the Bible translation process. The board also discussed the possibility of the Townsends' moving to Colombia to head up the SIL work there. Everything was going fine in Peru, and the work in Colombia had many challenges, especially since the country was not open to traditional missionary work.

Cam agreed to pray with Elaine about the move, and after the board meeting, he returned home to Peru. Soon after he got back, a visitor arrived from New York. Mrs. Magnuson had come to Peru on business, and a friend had told her to visit the SIL camp while she was in the country. Elaine Townsend had graciously offered to have her stay and observe the work SIL was doing with the Indians. Everything Mrs. Magnuson saw impressed her, especially the way the translators involved themselves in the daily lives of the native people.

At dinner on her last evening with the Townsends, Mrs. Magnuson said to Cam, "I don't mean to tell you what to do, but it seems to me everyone should know how you are helping these tribes. Have you ever thought about a pavilion at the New York World's Fair?"

Cam nearly dropped the baked sweet potato he had balanced on the end of his fork. He cleared his throat. "Well, actually," he began, "I have given it a little thought."

"So you're already on to it!" beamed Mrs. Magnuson. "I knew a man like you wouldn't miss such a golden opportunity. I happen to know the fair's manager. His name is Bob Moses, and I'm sure I could convince him to give you a free lot. Work like this needs to be promoted." She took a deep breath and continued. "Grace tells me you are taking her to North Carolina to attend school soon. If you come up to New York, I will introduce you to Bob Moses and get the ball rolling for you."

Three months later, Cameron Townsend found himself in New York City. He met with Cornell Capa, the famous *Life* magazine photographer who was producing a book titled *Who Brought the Word* for SIL. Cam discussed with him the idea of having a pavilion at the World's Fair, and Cornell told him he thought it was a great idea, provided they could raise the money.

With great anticipation and enthusiasm, Cam accompanied Mrs. Magnuson to meet Bob Moses, who sat quietly and listened as she gave a glowing account of SIL's work in Peru.

When it was Cam's turn to speak, he began telling Bob Moses about the plans he had dreamed up for the pavilion. "We could make it up to look like a jungle," he explained. "The public could walk along a jungle path with bird sounds and other animal noises playing in the background. Then they could go into a thatched hut and see a display of rare tribal artifacts. We would have our people on hand to discuss the items and answer any questions people might have about native tribes and the work we do with them."

"Wonderful idea!" exclaimed Bob. "We don't have anything like that planned. It would be a showstopper." He reached across his desk for a sheet of paper. "I'll tell you what I'll do, Mr. Townsend. I'll give you a free lot right smack in the middle of things." He surveyed the paper, which Cam could see was a map. "Right here's the spot for you. It's on the corner of the Avenue of America and the Avenue of Europe." He drew a ring around the lot and turned the page so that Cam could see it. "There," he said. "Every person who comes to the World's Fair will walk right past your pavilion."

Cam felt himself grinning from ear to ear. This was more than he had hoped for.

"Now," continued Bob, "you will need to have the money to put up the pavilion soon so that I can secure the spot for you, and the pavilion has to be ready to open in April."

"Yes," agreed Cam. "That sounds very fair. Thank you for all you have done for us. I'll have to okay this all with the board, of course, but I'll be back in touch with you as soon as possible to let you know if we can take advantage of your most generous offer."

The next day Mrs. Magnuson saw Cam off at the airport. Cam was flying to California, where a SIL board meeting was to be held.

Just as Cam was about to board the plane, Mrs. Magnuson pressed an envelope into his hand. "You must go ahead with the pavilion," she said.

Once the airplane had taken off, Cam opened the envelope. Inside was a check for a thousand dollars. He began to do some math in his head. Even without having to pay the two hundred fifty thousand dollars for the lot, Cam estimated it would cost about one hundred thousand dollars to set up the pavilion and staff it for two years. In his pocket was the first thousand dollars of that amount, but where would the rest come from?

Two days later, Cam had seven thousand dollars. A retired missionary couple who heard him speak at a church gave one thousand dollars, and five thousand dollars came from two of his relatives. Cam became more convinced than ever that the World's Fair pavilion should go ahead. Now it was time to convince the board.

Cam told the SIL board members all that had happened so far with regard to the pavilion. While some of them could see that it might be a good idea, no one was ready to break the organization's rules and borrow the money needed to make it happen. The debate went back and forth all morning long, until Cam came up with a possible solution. He leaned forward in his seat and looked at his friends around the table. "What if I found enough people who were willing and able to underwrite the project?" he asked.

As he looked around the table, Cam noticed one of the board members frowning, so he began explaining further what he meant. "I could ask some people if they would be willing to pay the shortfall if we didn't raise enough money between now and the end of the fair. I would hope that we can make enough money from book sales and donations during the fair to cover our costs. If we do, these underwriters wouldn't have to pay a penny. However, if we don't make enough to cover our costs, these people will have agreed in advance to make up the difference. What do you think?"

Cam waited eagerly as the board members looked from one person to another.

"Well," Ken Pike finally said, "we don't want to go into debt, but that wouldn't be debt, since we wouldn't be responsible to cover things if the money didn't come in. I think I could agree to that. What do you others think?"

Soon it was agreed that Cam should go ahead with the pavilion at the World's Fair, as long as he found enough individuals to underwrite the entire debt for building and running it.

Cam was excited to have the matter approved. In his mind he could already see the crowds streaming past the huge ten-foot-high, one-hundred-foot-long mural that would run the length of the pavilion.

As it turned out, the New York World's Fair was not the financial success Cam had hoped it would be, but in other ways it was very successful. By the end of 1964, a record number of 202 recruits had signed up to do translation work with SIL, bringing the organization's membership to sixteen hundred. That same year, over three million dollars was raised for the work of SIL, with nearly all of it going directly to missionaries working in tribal areas. Over one million people had stopped in at the pavilion, and two-thirds of them had taken the time to listen to a talk about SIL's work. Over one hundred newspapers and magazines had run articles that shared the needs of tribal people within the United States and around the world. Cam felt more than ever that the job of reaching every tribe and language with the gospel could be achieved in his lifetime.

Chapter 19

A Growing Organization

The years continued to roll by for Cam and Elaine Townsend. Their oldest daughter Grace married Tom Goreth in 1966. True to form, Cam used the opportunity to remind the 250 wedding guests that there were still two thousand tribes who had never heard the gospel in their own language.

That same year, Cam was awarded an honorary degree from the University of San Marcos in Peru. He had been offered other degrees by several well-known universities in the United States, but he had always turned them down, not wanting people to think a person had to have a degree to be a good translator. However, he decided to accept the degree from the university in Peru as a gesture of respect for the country's education system. Now, at seventy years of age, he was officially Dr. W. Cameron Townsend, though everybody still called him Uncle Cam.

Even as he got older, Cam never stopped looking for new tribes who needed to have the Bible translated for them. As he looked around, his gaze settled on a place that most Americans considered impossible to reach: the Caucasus region of the Soviet Union, located between the Black and Caspian Seas. Over one hundred separate languages were spoken in the region. The problem was that the people who spoke those languages—along with the people of Poland, Hungary, Romania, Bulgaria, Czechoslovakia and East Germany—were locked behind the "Iron Curtain." Not only were they behind the Iron Curtain, but the Soviet Union and the United States were still locked in a Cold War with each other. Indeed, there was so much mistrust between the two countries that it was virtually impossible for an American to get a visa to enter the Soviet Union.

Despite all of the political and ideological hatred and mistrust that existed between the two countries, Cam desperately wanted to find a way to bring the Bible to the millions of ethnic people in the Soviet Union who lived without any knowledge of the gospel. Many people told him it was an impossible dream, but the word *impossible* was not in Cam's vocabulary.

In 1967, Cam and Elaine moved to Mexico City, in part so that they could study Russian. They took lessons every day, and each day they prayed that God would open up a way for them to go to the Soviet Union. Cam made friends with many people from the Soviet embassy in Mexico City. He charmed them with stories from his years of adventure translating the Bible into native languages.

Finally, in the summer of 1968, Cam felt the time was right to ask for permission to visit the Soviet Union. He had to have a specific destination where he wanted to go in the country, so he wrote to the Soviet Academy of Science in Moscow, asking whether he could come to compare notes with Russian linguists.

It was September before he got the answer he was waiting for. He had an invitation to visit the academy as soon as he wanted. That was all Cam needed. He swung into action, telling Elaine he would like to be in Moscow within ten days. Thankfully, Elaine was used to her husband's fast decisions, and she spent all one day and most of the next on the phone informing more than eighty of their friends and supporters that the doors to the Soviet Union were open. They were about to fulfill Cam's dream of going behind the Iron Curtain.

Promises of prayer and money flowed in, and by the time Cam and Elaine were ready to leave on Wednesday, October 2, 1968, they had everything they needed. It was particularly hard for Elaine to think of leaving their four children, though the children were hardly little anymore. Grace had been married for two years, Joy and Elainadel were attending Columbia Bible College, and Bill was enjoying his time at Ben Lippen, a boarding high school.

Cam and Elaine left New York on a cold, blustery day and arrived in Moscow to an even colder blast of Arctic air. After living in Central America for so long, they found the freezing temperatures to be quite a shock. Even in their hotel room, which overlooked Red Square, the Townsends often kept their coats on for warmth.

Their first task in Moscow was to get a better grasp of the Russian language, so they studied for about six hours a day. The rest of the time they spent exploring Moscow or visiting the new friends they had made in the Mexican and Colombian embassies.

While Cam was in Moscow, he heard the legend that Russians used to explain why there were over one hundred distinct languages in the Caucasus. The legend said that as an angel flew over the area giving out languages, he flew too close to the cliff and ripped open the bottom of his bag on a sharp rock. As a result, languages tumbled out and settled on the valleys below, causing people who lived so closely together to speak so many different languages.

The legend fascinated Cam. He had never heard an explanation quite like it before. It made him want to get out into the countryside and get to know the people who spoke each of the different languages.

By Christmas, Cam and Elaine felt they knew enough Russian to get started with their real purpose for being in the Soviet Union. They took a train to the

Caucasus region and began visiting officials and other people there. They stopped at schools and universities, museums and factories, observing the good job the Soviet Union had done in helping to improve literacy in the most remote areas. Cam could see that just about everyone could read. Now the challenge was to find a way to translate the Bible into all of the various languages for people to read.

At first a number of officials were not pleased with Cam's plan and ideas. They pointed out that the Soviet Union, which was an atheist state, had no place for God. Cam found a way around the problem, however. One linguist Cam met with told him he would not be allowed to translate any part of the Bible into a local language. After thinking about it for a moment, though, the linguist then corrected himself. "We are allowed to write down ancient traditional stories, and Bible stories would fall into that category."

Cam nodded in agreement. He had found that there was always some way to translate the Bible, even in so-called closed countries. When Cam and Elaine returned to Moscow in February 1969, an official invitation was extended to SIL to come to the Soviet Union to work with the languages of the Caucasus region. Thanks to Cam's diplomacy and track record working in other countries, SIL was one of the few foreign organizations ever invited to work in the Soviet Union.

Of course, when the Townsends got back to the United States, everyone was eager to hear about the open door into the Soviet Union. Elaine set off on a thirty-day tour that took her from the East Coast to the West Coast, with forty-eight stops along the way. While she did this, Cam flew to Mexico City for the dedication of SIL's new regional headquarters building. SIL had outgrown "The Kettle," and so a new building had been erected to replace it. The building housed offices, a computer room, a library, an auditorium, and a small museum displaying tribal artifacts. The rooms were named after the various officials who had helped SIL during its thirty-two years of work in Mexico.

The biennial conference of SIL was held in the new facility. When it was over, Cam headed back to Charlotte, North Carolina, where he and Elaine had agreed to build a permanent home, or as permanent as any home the Townsends had lived in. Soon after his arrival in Charlotte, Cam announced plans to return to the Soviet Union. He wanted to write a book about how bilingual education had improved the life of people in the Caucasus. He also thought he might visit some of the SIL workers in Asia and the Pacific region. Although Cam prayed each day for the Wycliffe Bible translators spread around the world, he had not seen many of the places where they worked.

By the beginning of October 1969, everything was set. Cam and Elaine, accompanied by sixteen-year-old Bill, boarded an airplane bound for the Soviet Union. Cam intended to spend a month there collecting photographs and information for his book.

In Moscow, Cam received a hearty welcome. The Soviet leaders were right behind his idea for a book, and they assigned a government photographer to accompany him to the Caucasus. The month flew by as Cam visited schools and universities throughout the region. Everywhere he went he asked officials how they had managed to increase literacy among the poorest people.

When the month was up, it was time for the Townsends to fly on to New Delhi, India, and then to Nepal, where Cam was greatly impressed by the work he saw. Fifteen SIL workers from six different nations were working on translating twelve local languages. Students from Nepal's only university were working alongside them. This was exactly what Cam had wanted SIL to be thirty-six years before when he had founded the organization. He wanted it to be an organization made up of people from many countries who fanned out across the globe, translating the Bible and cooperating with government officials wherever they could.

The Philippines was the next port of call. Here, once again, Cam was greatly moved by the dedication of the Wycliffe workers. One hundred fifty-six of them were working with forty-two native languages. There was nothing Cam would have liked more than to roll up his sleeves and join the workers, but he had to get back to the United States and focus on his Soviet studies.

From the Philippines, Cam and Elaine went to Papua New Guinea. SIL was working hard in this forgotten corner of the world. Over three hundred translators were in the country working on translating the Bible into eighty-seven tribal languages. They had also followed the example Cam had set in Tetelcingo, Mexico, more than thirty years before. There Cam had helped the people of the village improve their daily lives by showing them how to irrigate and grow new crops. Al Pence, the director of SIL in Papua New Guinea, proudly showed Cam how native men were now running a print shop and a lumber mill. Not only that, but many of the young men had been trained in a variety of technical skills.

From Papua New Guinea, the Townsends visited Australia and New Zealand before heading back to the United States via Hawaii.

When they got back to North Carolina, Elaine made an appointment for Cam to see a doctor. Once or twice towards the end of their trip, Cam had noticed that he was short of breath. Elaine was worried that it might be something serious, but Cam pointed out that he was now seventy-three years old and had been traveling through time zones at a rapid rate, speaking and visiting with people everywhere he went. That was enough to take the breath away from a man half his age!

Still Elaine got her way, and the doctor frowned when Cam described his shortness of breath and chest pains. An appointment was made with a heart specialist. Sure enough, the specialist told Cam he had heart problems. He also said the best treatment for the ailment was for Cam to slow down.

For the first time ever, Cam took a doctor's advice seriously. He tried hard not to be too busy, but there was a new yard to tend and hundreds of people all over the world to keep in touch with. And then there was the book about Soviet bilingual education to write. Slowing down was not easy for Cam, but by now he had accepted that it was time to leave most of his SIL work in the capable hands of the next generation.

Cam was very happy when their second daughter, Joy, married in June 1970. Joy and her husband, David Tuggy, joined SIL and went to Mexico to finish the work Cam had begun on the Aztec New Testament years before.

Still, after a lifetime of pushing ahead with his plans, Cam could not sit around and do nothing. He forged on with an idea he'd had for a long time to get the United States government to recognize the work that still needed to be done among native-speaking groups. President Nixon, a Quaker himself, had for many years shown an interest in the work of SIL. Cam had a presidential aide present a resolution to Congress declaring 1971 as the "Year of Minority Language Groups." The resolution passed in both the House and the Senate, and President Nixon signed the proclamation.

On December 2, 1970, Cam found himself in the Oval Office of the White House along with several senators and President Nixon. Everyone listened attentively as Cam explained that SIL workers had just begun translation work on their five hundredth language. President Nixon was very impressed.

Cam left the White House that snowy day with a warm feeling inside. It seemed almost unbelievable as he thought back over the years and all the opportunities he'd had to work with presidents and high government officials. He thought, too, of his old friend Lázaro Cárdenas, the ex-president of Mexico, who had died two months before. Cam had rushed down to his funeral, wanting to honor a friend who had done so much to help SIL get established in its early days.

Several days after his visit to the White House, Cam received an official letter on presidential stationery. He eagerly read the letter. After thanking Cam for visiting the White House, President Nixon went on to say:

> I was honored to have you at the White House and interested in learning of the difficult and challenging efforts of your group in translating the Bible for the multitudes throughout the world who are deprived of a common language. I am happy to have this opportunity to commend all the linguists and other personnel who are dedicated to this worthy task.
>
> With my appreciation and best wishes for success in reaching your desired goals.
>
> Sincerely,
>
> Richard Nixon

It was a wonderful moment for Cam, not because he had personally been recognized by the president of the United States but because the commendation meant that more people would consider joining SIL, and SIL needed all the workers it could get!

Soon after his visit to the White House, Cam made a decision: It was time for him to resign as general director of Wycliffe Bible Translators/SIL. Cam chose to make the announcement at SIL's biennial business meeting in Mexico City in May 1971.

It was a poignant moment when Ben Elson, the organization's executive director, read the annual report. SIL now had 2,504 workers doing translation work in 510 languages spread among 23 countries. The annual income for the organization was an astonishing 7.9 million dollars.

It would have been easy for Cam to sit back and congratulate himself on the amazing success of the organization he had started, but that was not Cam's way. Cam was always looking forward to the next challenge, the next people group who needed the Bible translated into their language. When it was his time to speak, Cam cleared his throat and began: "God has been good to us. He led us into our unusual policies. Let's be true to them. Let's forge ahead until every tribe has heard the Word of God in its own tongue."

It was the same message Cam had preached for fifty-four years, everywhere from the tiniest church to his own daughter's wedding. And more than that, it was the message he had lived every day of his life.

Chapter 20

The Work Goes On

Cam may have resigned as general director of SIL, but he still did what he could. He finished his book on Soviet bilingual education, titled *They Found a Common Language: Community Through Bilingual Education*. The publication of the book opened the door for Cam and Elaine to make several trips back to the Soviet Union.

Cam also continued to travel to other places, though at a slower pace. In 1973, the president of Pakistan invited him to speak on bilingual education. This was followed by an invitation from India's prime minister, Indira Gandhi, to visit her country. There were many awards, too, each of which Cam accepted on behalf of all the SIL workers. The president of the Philippines gave Cam a citation, and Cam received the highest honor given to foreigners in both Mexico and Peru.

In 1979, UNESCO gave the Summer Institute of Linguistics a literacy award for its excellent work in Papua New Guinea. Every summer since 1934, SIL programs had been held, but soon after receiving the UNESCO award, this changed. The Summer Institute of Linguistics outgrew its name. A group of Christian businessmen donated land for a permanent, year-round facility, and SIL moved from being a summer program to one that trained translators year-round.

Other centers within the United States began springing up. And the Jungle Aviation and Radio Service continued to add to its facility near Charlotte, North Carolina, twenty-five miles from where Cam and Elaine now lived.

Nineteen seventy-nine was a great year for Cam and SIL. It was the year the Amuesha tribe in Peru received the New Testament in its own language. Any translation thrilled Cam, but the Amuesha translation brought him particular joy. It was the one hundredth New Testament translation completed by SIL workers.

There was even more encouragement for Cam. Ken Pike, who began his tenure in SIL as a skinny, sickly looking student, had always been on the cutting edge of linguistic research. In 1942, he had earned his Ph.D. in linguistics from the University of Michigan. Over the years, he had been awarded honorary doctorates from six well-known American universities, and in 1981, he, along with the Summer Institute of Linguistics, was nominated for the Nobel Peace Prize for work among the ethnic minorities of the world. Cam could not have been more pleased, especially for his old student. Ken Pike had been a strong member of the SIL team from the first day.

During Christmas season 1981, Cam began to feel unusually weak. Elaine urged him to go to the doctor, which he did. The diagnosis was not good. Cameron Townsend was suffering from acute leukemia. There was no cure for the disease, but having repeated blood transfusions seemed to help patients live a little longer. Between January and April 1982, Cam received eighteen blood transfusions.

In March, Cam and Elaine were able to stay in a friend's house in Florida. Everyone knew that Cam was not expected to live long, and many people asked to visit him one last time. Elaine set up an appointment schedule for him, and Cam was able to spend an hour each with twenty-five of his old friends. He and Elaine stayed in Florida for a month and then returned to their home near Charlotte. Cam had been home a week when his condition worsened. Elaine took him to the hospital, where he died peacefully on April 23, 1982. He was eighty-five years old.

Telegrams and phone calls began pouring in from all over the world. Presidents telephoned to offer their sympathy, and peasants Cam had personally taught to read and write wrote letters of condolence to Elaine and the family.

Thousands of people mourned the loss of their beloved Uncle Cam. Through the tears, there was also thanks for all that Cameron Townsend, the freckle-faced young kid born into a poor farming family, had been able to achieve during his lifetime.

The funeral service was held at Calvary Church in Charlotte, and William Cameron Townsend was buried at the nearby JAARS headquarters. The inscription on his gravestone read, "Dear Ones: By love serve one another. Finish the task. Translate the Scriptures into every language."

After the funeral service, more than a hundred people stayed behind at JAARS headquarters. They sang hymns and told stories about Uncle Cam far into the night.

One friend retold a story that had happened many years before. He had been listening to Cam talk about his vision of seeing the Bible translated into every language on earth. A bit taken aback, the man had said, "Cam, I don't see how it will be possible for you to get working arrangements for your project in Buddhist, Muslim, and Communist countries. It's wonderful that you've been able to serve in Latin America, but I don't see how you can go into these other countries." According to the friend, Cam had turned to him with a smile and said, "I don't see how we can fail if we trust God and follow His leadership. 'All power is given unto Me in heaven and on earth,' declared our Lord. 'Go ye therefore.'"

Cam had lived his life according to those words. He had spent his days sharing with others the vision of translating the Bible into every language on earth and training people to go and do just that. It was not surprising that after his death the work went on.

Today Wycliffe Bible Translators/SIL workers have completed translating the New Testament in five hundred languages and are currently working on translating it into another thousand languages. However, there are still four hundred forty million people in two thousand people groups who do not have the New Testament in their own language. SIL's goal is to begin translation of the Bible into all remaining languages in the next twenty-five years.

Following Cam's death, Elaine Townsend made several more trips around the world promoting the goals of SIL and encouraging the workers. She still loves to speak to the new recruits and is actively involved in SIL prayer groups, as well as keeping track of her four children and nineteen grandchildren. Cam and Elaine's first great-grandchild was a girl. Her parents named her Cameron in honor of the person whose life goal was to translate the Good News in every language.

Bibliography

Hefley, James and Marti. *Uncle Cam*. Wycliffe Bible Translators, 1984.

Steven, Hugh. *A Thousand Trails*. CREDO Publishing Corporation, 1984.

Townsend, William Cameron, and Richard S. Pittman. *Remember All the Way*. Wycliffe Bible Translators, 1975.

Wallis, Ethel Emily, and Mary Angela Bennett. *Two Thousand Tongues to Go: The Story of the Wycliffe Bible Translators*. Harper & Brothers, 1959.

Janet and Geoff Benge are a husband and wife writing team with more than twenty years of writing experience. Janet is a former elementary school teacher. Geoff holds a degree in history. Originally from New Zealand, the Benges spent ten years serving with Youth With A Mission. They have two daughters, Laura and Shannon, and an adopted son, Lito. They make their home in the Orlando, Florida, area.

Also from Janet and Geoff Benge...

Christian Heroes: Then & Now

Gladys Aylward: The Adventure of a Lifetime • 978-1-57658-019-6

Nate Saint: On a Wing and a Prayer • 978-1-57658-017-2

Hudson Taylor: Deep in the Heart of China • 978-1-57658-016-5

Amy Carmichael: Rescuer of Precious Gems • 978-1-57658-018-9

Eric Liddell: Something Greater Than Gold • 978-1-57658-137-7

Corrie ten Boom: Keeper of the Angels' Den • 978-1-57658-136-0

William Carey: Obliged to Go • 978-1-57658-147-6

George Müller: Guardian of Bristol's Orphans • 978-1-57658-145-2

Jim Elliot: One Great Purpose • 978-1-57658-146-9

Mary Slessor: Forward into Calabar • 978-1-57658-148-3

David Livingstone: Africa's Trailblazer • 978-1-57658-153-7

Betty Greene: Wings to Serve • 978-1-57658-152-0

Adoniram Judson: Bound for Burma • 978-1-57658-161-2

Cameron Townsend: Good News in Every Language • 978-1-57658-164-3

Jonathan Goforth: An Open Door in China • 978-1-57658-174-2

Lottie Moon: Giving Her All for China • 978-1-57658-188-9

John Williams: Messenger of Peace • 978-1-57658-256-5

William Booth: Soup, Soap, and Salvation • 978-1-57658-258-9

Rowland Bingham: Into Africa's Interior • 978-1-57658-282-4

Ida Scudder: Healing Bodies, Touching Hearts • 978-1-57658-285-5

Wilfred Grenfell: Fisher of Men • 978-1-57658-292-3

Lillian Trasher: The Greatest Wonder in Egypt • 978-1-57658-305-0

Loren Cunningham: Into All the World • 978-1-57658-199-5

Florence Young: Mission Accomplished • 978-1-57658-313-5

Sundar Singh: Footprints Over the Mountains • 978-1-57658-318-0

C. T. Studd: No Retreat • 978-1-57658-288-6

Rachel Saint: A Star in the Jungle • 978-1-57658-337-

Brother Andrew: God's Secret Agent • 978-1-57658-355-5

Clarence Jones: Mr. Radio • 978-1-57658-343-2

Count Zinzendorf: Firstfruit • 978-1-57658-262-6

John Wesley: The World His Parish • 978-1-57658-382-1

C. S. Lewis: Master Storyteller • 978-1-57658-385-2

David Bussau: Facing the World Head-on • 978-1-57658-415-6

Jacob DeShazer: Forgive Your Enemies • 978-1-57658-475-0

Isobel Kuhn: On the Roof of the World • 978-1-57658-497-2

Elisabeth Elliot: Joyful Surrender • 978-1-57658-513-9

Paul Brand: Helping Hands • 978-1-57658-536-8

D. L. Moody: Bringing Souls to Christ • 978-1-57658-552-8